THE Dark Side OF THE SUPER-NATURAL

BILL MYERS AND DAVID WIMBISH

THE Dark Side OF THE SUPER- NATURAL

BETHANY HOUSE PUBLISHERS
MINNEAPOLIS, MINNESOTA 55438

Published by Bethany House Publishers
A Ministry of Bethany Fellowship International
11400 Hampshire Avenue South
Minneapolis, Minnesota 55438
www.bethanyhouse.com

Printed in the United States of America by
Bethany Press International, Minneapolis, Minnesota 55438

Library of Congress Cataloging-in-Publication Data

Myers, Bill, 1953–
    The dark side of the supernatural / by Bill Myers and David Wimbish.
    p. cm.

    ISBN 0–7642–2151–5 (pbk.)
    1. Occultism—Religious aspects—Christianity. I. Wimbish, David.
II. Title.
    BR115.O3 M94 1999
    261.5'13—dc21   99–6637
                                                          CIP

For Diane:
An inspiration to us both

Bethany House Books by

Bill Myers

Journeys to Fayrah
CHILDREN'S ALLEGORICAL SERIES
> The Portal
> The Experiment
> The Whirlwind
> The Tablet

Bloodhounds, Inc.
CHILDREN'S MYSTERY SERIES
> The Ghost of KRZY
> The Mystery of the Invisible Knight
> Phantom of the Haunted Church
> Invasion of the UFOs
> Fangs for the Memories
> Case of the Missing Minds

Nonfiction
> The Dark Side of the Supernatural
> Hot Topics, Tough Questions

Bill Myers' website: www.BillMyers.com

BILL MYERS is the bestselling author of more than fifty books—including *Blood of Heaven, Threshold,* and *Fire of Heaven*—that bring Christian insight into the world of the supernatural. He is the beloved co-creator of "McGee and Me."

DAVID WIMBISH is the author or co-writer of more than twenty books and has more than twenty-five years' experience as a reporter, television writer, and creative supervisor in a national advertising firm.

Contents

1

Something Strange
Is Going on Here

"Reach out in the darkness, and you might find a friend."
That's what the old song says to do.

And that's what millions of people *are* trying to do.

They're reaching into the darkness of the supernatural realm hoping to find "a friend." They're looking for angels. Seeking to contact the dead. Having encounters with beings who claim to be 35,000-year-old spirits. Engaging in automatic writing and other forms of "spirit communication." Conversing with beings who claim to have come from distant galaxies to give us a helping hand.

Maybe you remember the scene from the movie *E.T.* where Elliott's ball rolls into a backyard shed. The little boy is just about to go in to retrieve it when it rolls back out. Intrigued—and a bit frightened—he rolls it into the shed a second time . . . and again it comes bouncing back out. Now

Elliott's really scared, because he knows there's someone—or perhaps something—in there.

Today, all over the world, people are rolling balls into the darkness to see if anyone is out there.

And someone is rolling them back.

Someone. But who?

Are we making contact with friendly beings who want to help us? Or is the answer far more sinister?

INTO THE DEPTHS

As we begin our search for answers to these questions, let me tell you about Mark.

Like many of us, Mark had much too much to do. He was running as fast as he could, only to find that at the end of each day he was further behind. The stress became so bad he couldn't sleep more than a few hours at night. He lost his appetite. He felt a constant tightness in his chest and a burning sensation in his stomach.

When he told a co-worker how he was feeling, the man suggested he try a form of Eastern meditation. His friend told him he had tried this kind of meditation himself, and it had calmed him down, given him a more positive outlook, and helped him to cope with day-to-day frustrations.

It sounded great. Even though Mark seemed to remember somewhere in the back of his mind that this form of meditation involved "mystical" religious practices, that didn't really bother him. He was ready to try anything, and he figured that meditation had to be better than a daily dose of Prozac.

Mark found that meditation was everything his co-worker said it would be. Almost immediately, he felt renewed and relaxed. He meditated as often as he could . . . even at work. He could close the door of his office, recite his mantra, and leave his worries behind. Even though Mark was a dedicated Christian, he wondered how he had ever managed to get through life without meditation.

At his deepest, most peaceful moments, he felt he had made contact with benevolent spirits from beyond this world—beings that were beautiful, loving, full of joy and peace.

Mark practiced to the point where it was easy to slip into a dreamlike state. It was almost like a trance.

And that's when he had the vision.

On a quiet, still evening, all alone in his living room, Mark had an encounter with something evil. Something that had been waiting for him in the depths of his meditation experiences.

Mark wasn't so sure it was just a vision. To him, the creature was suddenly in the room with him, mocking him and daring him to try to regain control of his life.

"I was aware," he said, "that I was falling into the grip of someone I didn't want to even touch me."

Was it Satan?

"If it wasn't, it came pretty darn close."

13

Why did the "creature" choose that moment to reveal himself?

"I have no idea. Maybe they figured I was so far gone that they had me, so they had nothing to lose by revealing themselves to me."

"*Themselves?*"

"The ones who are behind it all. Satan and his demons."

TERROR IN INDIANA

Some people might be tempted to think that what happened to Mark was an isolated incident or the product of an overactive imagination.

Perhaps. But his experience resembles too many others. Take Bill Fogarty, for example.

Fogarty was a student at the Indiana University in the early 1970s when he became involved in a weekly "discussion" group with several friends searching for spiritual truth. At first, they talked about all sorts of things—politics, philosophy, literature, whatever caught their interest. But as time went on, they found their attention turned more and more often to the "deeper mysteries" of life—specifically UFOs.

The five members of the group were all nondrinkers. They didn't do drugs. They weren't prone to hysteria or hallucinations, drug induced or otherwise. They were physically fit young men who were doing well in school.

But as the group's interest in UFOs intensified, they

began to openly seek contact with "other-worldly" beings. That's when strange things began to happen. That's when they began to see lights in the night sky. Later, according to Fogarty, they heard "rappings in the dark, hollow voices, heavy breathing, and the crushing footsteps of unseen entities."[1]

Initially, the five young men felt "honored" that they had been chosen for such experiences. They believed that because they were "rational and intelligent men," they could deal with anything that happened.

They were wrong.

The nocturnal rapping became violent pounding. One group member was struck hard in the face by an invisible hand. Another young man reported that he couldn't sleep because unseen forces shook and bounced his bed all night long. One of the students awakened in the middle of the night to find strange "dark-clad men" staring down at him.

They all had the feeling they were being followed. Radios and TV sets switched on and off, even though nobody was close to them. Securely locked doors opened and then closed again.

Fogarty began sleeping with the light on. He kept a gun under his pillow.

One of his friends "invested heavily in weapons and began running with a group that offered sacrifices to Odin," the ancient Viking god of storms and death.

Two others dropped out of school a month before they would have graduated with honors.[2]

Like Mark, their forays into the occult had not produced the results they desired.

A HUNGER FOR THE SUPERNATURAL

Human beings are spiritual creatures. We hunger for an encounter with the spiritual. We seem to know instinctively that there is more to this life than what we are able to experience with our five physical senses. Implanted in all of us is a desire to understand the ultimate meaning of things. We want to know that the daily grind isn't really "all there is" to our existence.

Man has always had an interest in the supernatural. But we live in an age in which that interest has become extreme. Everywhere we turn, there are books and other materials related to mysticism and the occult. There are dozens of psychic telephone lines, hundreds of authors and lecturers who claim to "channel" departed spirits, and "New Age" books and other materials in every bookstore. Then there are thousands of Web sites dedicated to occult issues.

Obviously, millions of people are turning to occult practices for answers to life's questions. But one wonders if they should trust the answers they get . . . or the ones who give those answers.

Judging by the thousands of experiences of the Marks and the Bill Fogartys of the world, the answer appears to be a resounding "No!"

As these and hundreds of other stories show, it can be

incredibly dangerous to press into the supernatural dark-ness—especially without the benefit of a light to show the way. And as we will see, there is no greater light than the Word of God—the Bible.

In the chapters ahead, we will seek to shine that light on a number of current "spiritual" beliefs and practices and see what our attitude toward them should be.

SHOULD WE BE CURIOUS? OR CAUTIOUS?

Now, you may think that most occult occurrences are flat-out hoaxes—or the work of overactive imaginations. And do you know what? So do I. Most supernatural tales are like mist. They vanish into nothing when you try to touch them. But there are occasional occurrences that defy rational explanation. They hold up under careful investigation: *There are* haunted locations where chains rattle and disembodied voices can be heard whispering in the night. *There are* people who receive messages from "beyond" through trances, au-tomatic writing, and other means. *There are* strange craft of unknown origin zipping through our skies.

And if we know the source of these strange happenings, we will probably be a lot less curious about them—and a lot more cautious.

The fact is this: Satan is alive and well, and he is doing everything within his power to draw people away from God. He seeks to convince us that the Bible is old and outdated, that there are newer and better truths that can lead the human race to freedom, enlightenment, and fulfillment. Yet God says, "Heaven and earth will pass away, but my words will never pass away" (Luke 21:33). He also warns us that in the last days, "false Christs and false prophets will appear and perform great signs and miracles to deceive even the elect—if that were possible" (Matt. 24:24).

The book of Second Thessalonians contains an even stronger warning:

> The coming of the lawless one will be in accordance with the work of Satan displayed in all kinds of counterfeit miracles, signs and wonders, and in every sort of evil that deceives those who are perishing. They perish because they refused to love the truth and so be saved. For this reason, God sends them a powerful delusion . . . (2:9–11)

SATAN: MR. PREDICTABLE!

Some of today's most popular beliefs are grouped together under the banner of the "New Age Movement." But that's a misnomer. There is nothing at all "new" about these beliefs. In fact, Satan really hasn't changed much over the centuries. He still comes to us with the lie he used on Adam and Eve in the Garden of Eden. "Eat . . . your eyes will be opened, and you will be like God, knowing good and evil" (Gen. 3:4).

Today he makes the same promise: "Eat of my fruit and

you will be like God. In fact, you *are* God. You will simply learn to release that God part of you that is locked within."

It's the same old lie, but with a slightly different spin for modern audiences.

Before we get further into our investigation of supernatural experiences, we need to remember two points:

First, it would be wise to recall the excellent advice of C. S. Lewis: "There are two equal and opposite errors into which our race can fall about devils. One is to disbelieve in their existence. The other is to believe, and to feel an excessive and unhealthy interest in them."[3]

Lewis spoke of devils, but he could just as easily have been referring to an unhealthy interest in the occult. Yes, it is important to have our spiritual eyes and ears opened, to be *aware* of what Satan is doing in the world today.

Aware of it, yes. *Fascinated by it*, no.

The purpose of this book isn't to draw undue attention to Satan or to bring him glory. It is to expose him as the deceiving coward and fraud that he is and to show how his tricks and magic pale in comparison to the true creative power that comes only from the hand of God.

The second point to remember is this:

Even though there is danger in the world of the occult, there is no power anywhere that can begin to come close to rivaling the power of God or His Word. If you are a child of God, there is nothing Satan and all the powers of darkness can do to harm you.

Jesus said of those who belong to Him that "no one can

snatch them out of my hand. My Father, who has given them to me, is greater than all; no one can snatch them out of my Father's hand" (John 10:28–29).

He also promised that those who belong to Him would be given the power and authority to prevail against the supernatural powers of darkness:

> "These signs will accompany those who believe: In my name they will drive out demons" (Mark 16:17).
>
> The one who is in you is greater than the one who is in the world. (1 John 4:4)
>
> "I tell you the truth, anyone who has faith in me will do what I have been doing. He will do even greater things than these" (John 14:12).

Would we recognize these powers of darkness if we came face-to-face with them? Would we be able to confront them with the power and authority that comes to us through Jesus Christ?

That's what this book hopes to do: Expose today's supernatural counterfeits and equip us to confront them and be victorious over them.

2

The Truth About Angels

Angels are everywhere these days. Angel pins. Angel books. Angel music. Angel TV shows.

In his book *Angels, Angels, Angels,* Phil Phillips points out:

> There was a time when we only made angels in snowdrifts, baked cookies in the shape of angels, topped Christmas trees with angel ornaments, or dressed our children in white sheets so they might be angels in Christmas pageants. No longer. Angels are now a year-round and highly profitable business phenomenon.[1]

Phillips quotes a *Time* magazine survey that reveals 46 percent of Americans believe they have their own guardian angel. A good number of folks are undecided, but only 21 percent don't believe in guardian angels at all.

All this, of course, is good.

Isn't it?

After all, angels are heavenly creatures. The Bible mentions angels more than 300 times, and the word "angel" comes from the Greek word *angelos*, or "messenger." Heralding messages from God is, in fact, one of the primary functions angels perform in God's kingdom. It was an angel who told Mary she would give birth to the Messiah. Angels sang in the skies over Bethlehem to announce the Savior's birth the night Christ was born. An angel will sound the last trumpet, proclaiming the day of God's judgment.

Aren't all angels by nature pure, holy, and completely above suspicion?

Well, as a matter of fact—according to the Bible—they aren't.

ANGEL OF LIGHT

The Bible states that Satan himself was once a high-ranking angel and that he is still capable of showing himself as an angel of light. (See 2 Cor. 11:14.)

Although the Bible doesn't provide great detail on the topic, several Scriptures indicate that somewhere back in time Satan led a revolt against God.

Apparently, Satan's chief sin has always been pride. He had status. He had standing. But it wasn't enough. Somehow he used his clout to get one-third of all the angels to join with him in an attempt to overthrow God himself! The book of Revelation puts it this way:

> And there was war in heaven. Michael and his angels fought against the dragon, and the dragon and his angels fought back. But he was not strong enough, and they lost their place in heaven. The great dragon was hurled down—that ancient serpent called the devil, or Satan, who leads the whole world astray. He was hurled to earth, and his angels with him. (Rev. 12:7–9)

GOOD GUYS AND BAD GUYS

According to the Bible, there are lots of good angels. But there are also bad angels. Some are *very* bad angels. What makes it even worse is that at least at first glance, it's impossible to tell them apart.

Satan and his angels don't wear red tights. They don't run around with pitchforks. They don't have horns sprouting out of the tops of their heads or bats' wings protruding from their backs. Interestingly enough, the only physical description I can recall of Satan in Scripture is as that "angel of light."

Now let's go back to the question we asked at the start of this chapter: Isn't it great that there are angels all over the place these days?

It all depends upon what kind of angels they are. If they're God's angels, it's wonderful. If they're angels following Satan, it's not so wonderful.

Don't misunderstand. I don't think there's anything wrong with wearing an angel, collecting angel figurines or paintings, or reading angel books . . . as long as we go to the Bible and double-check what those books say. Unfortunately, when we consult the Bible it seems that much of what's proclaimed these days directly contradicts God's Word. As a result, many people are buying lies about angels. And in some cases they're even opening themselves up to evil influences.

ANGEL WORSHIP

There's great danger in thinking of angels as something they are not and in looking to them as authorities in areas where they have none. And it's especially dangerous when a natural and healthy awe of angels grows into full-fledged worship. The Bible is clear in its teaching that angels are not to be worshiped. In fact, any angel who encourages or accepts our worship of him is not to be trusted.

Ever.

The apostle Paul warned against the worship of angels when he wrote, "Do not let anyone who delights in . . . the worship of angels disqualify you for the prize [of salvation through Christ]" (Col. 2:18).

In the book of Revelation, the apostle John tells what happened when he attempted to worship an angel who appeared to him: "I fell at his feet to worship him. But he said to me, 'Do not do it! I am a fellow servant with you and with your brothers who hold to the testimony of Jesus. Worship God!' " (Rev. 19:10).

MY "ENCOUNTER"

As a young man just out of college, I received a telephone call from a gentleman who claimed he was in constant contact with angels. It would have been easy to dismiss him as someone who needed a good therapist, except he was somewhat of a psychic celebrity and used these "angels" to help the police solve baffling crimes. In fact, he even told me that my telephone number had come to him in a dream.

As we talked, he told me that the angels sometimes spoke through him, and he offered to let me speak to one of them. I agreed. Immediately, his voice changed—completely. It became stronger, deeper, more authoritative.

Being young and naïve, I was excited by this possibility and remember putting my hand over the mouthpiece and whispering to my wife, "I think I'm talking to an angel!"

Over the next couple of days, I had more conversations with this fellow and several of his "angels." Was he faking it? I didn't think so. Each entity that spoke through him was so unique, with its own voice and distinctive way of speaking, that I felt certain I was talking to several different beings. Besides, they told me things about myself they couldn't have known except through supernatural means. They knew, for instance, that I was an aspiring writer. In fact, one of the voices assured me that I was going to be a successful author, and that I was going to accomplish great things for God through my writing. Of course, this was what I wanted to hear! The "angels" went out of their way to feed my pride and tantalize me with visions of glory. They constantly flattered me and made me feel I was somebody special.

They also seemed eager to help me achieve this fame by offering to help me write a book proclaiming the "deeper mysteries of God's love."

I grew uneasy. I didn't know much about angels then, but I began to suspect that these beings didn't really have my best interest in mind. They were a bit too slick. And instead of encouraging me to grow in humility and love, I sensed them stirring up my pride and desire for success.

Finally, I decided to ask one of these beings a crucial question: "Is Jesus Christ your Lord?"

"Absolutely!" he said. But before I could even breathe a sigh of relief, he added, "In fact, not only is He my Lord. He's also my brother."

I could feel the hair on the back of my neck rise.

Why? Because I knew Satan and his demons have always been driven by a desire to be considered God's equals. In fact, the Bible says, "You said in your heart, 'I will ascend to heaven; I will raise my throne above the stars of God . . . but you are brought down to the grave, to the depths of the pit'" (Isa. 14:12–15).

Satan and his angels are so full of pride that they simply can't help themselves. If they see a chance to equate themselves with God, they go for it.

I knew then that I wasn't talking with angels. I was dealing with demons. And once they realized I had caught on to their identity, their attitude toward me changed completely. At first, they tried to reason with me, but their reasoning had a sharp, sarcastic edge to it. They wondered how I could be so narrow-minded, and why I insisted on clinging so stubbornly to my outdated beliefs. When I wouldn't give in, they took to insulting me, saying that I was stupid, calling me names, and behaving in ways that didn't exactly fit the angel personality profile.

There's much more to the story, but I'll save it for later. Right now, the point I want to make is that the beings who spoke through this man were most definitely *not* the angels they claimed to be.

After my "close encounter" with fallen angels, I had a new appreciation for the Bible's words in the eighth chapter of Romans: "For I am convinced that neither death nor life, neither angels nor demons, neither the present nor the future, nor any powers, neither height nor depth, nor anything else in all creation, will be able to separate us from the love of God that is in Christ Jesus our Lord" (vv. 38–39). I had never before understood the part about angels trying to separate us from the love of God. Why would they want to do that? It seems clear to me now that true angels wouldn't. Fallen angels, or other beings masquerading as angels, would like nothing better.

THERE'S A WHOLE LOTTA LYIN' GOIN' ON

Today, as I look through some of the most popular books on angels, I see right away that I'm not the only one who has been lied to. When I check what these books say against the Bible, it becomes obvious that they are full of lies and dangerous half-truths:

- When an angel seeks to draw attention to himself and not to God, he is no angel.
- When an angel gladly accepts the adoration of men and women, you can be sure that he didn't come to us from heaven.
- When an angel tells us that he will answer our prayers and give us what we desire, he is attempting to usurp God's authority, and he is not to be trusted.
- When an angel tells us that we can be equal to God, he is no angel.

And yet the angels described in the pages of many current bestsellers do all of these things and more.

Author Phillips says that before he began writing *Angels, Angels, Angels*, he bought more than $500 worth of current books on the subject. He found that 90 percent of those books contained teachings about angels—who they are and what they do—that aren't consistent with the Bible.

My own experience is that Phillips' 90 percent figure may be low.

SATAN'S THREE FAVORITE LIES

Over and over again in this literature, three "angelic messages" keep coming through. They're the same three lies Satan has been selling to gullible people since he first encountered Adam and Eve in the Garden:

1. Christ is not the only begotten Son of God—and other teachers and angels are on a par with Him.

2. There are many paths to peace with God—and so Christ's death on the cross wasn't really necessary.

3. We all have within us the innate power to become like God—if only we would learn how to unleash it.

None of these statements agrees in the least with what the Bible teaches.

Some of the angel books I've read are particularly dangerous because they start out with sound biblical teaching, but give it a spin here and a twist there until nothing of the truth is left. They contain language familiar to most Christians—and that helps give even the most deceptive statements a ring of truth.

As Phillips writes, this has "opened the door for many Christians to be sucked in. Whereas Christians could once readily identify and reject New Age teaching because of the emphasis on reincarnation, the new emphasis on angels . . . has a much closer alignment with what many Christians *think* they have grown up believing. What they don't understand is that the New Age understanding of . . . angels is far different than the one they learned in Sunday school."[2]

WHAT DO THESE ANGELS WANT?

Linda Georgian of the Psychic Friends Network is a big fan of angels. In her book *Your Guardian Angels*, she writes that you don't have to subscribe to any particular religion to get help from angels, and adds that as she matured in her understanding of spiritual matters, she cast off her narrow-minded Christian (Catholic) upbringing. She says that just about anyone can learn to converse with angels, who are "always trying" to find an opening in our subconscious so they can communicate with us.

But why? What is it that they want to teach us?

To answer that question, let me tell you about a couple of famous men who have listened to angels. The first is Muhammad, the founder of Islam. Did you know that Islam was founded on the teaching of angels? According to Muhammad, it was the angel Gabriel who appeared to him and taught him that Christians have things all mixed up.

I don't believe Gabriel really appeared to Muhammad. But Muhammad thought he did, and so does the 20 percent of the earth's population that follows his teachings. And yet there is simply no way Islam and Christianity can both be right. They are diametrically opposed to each other.

Another man who listened to angels was a fellow named Joseph Smith.

One night, when he was twenty-five years old and contemplating what to do with the rest of his life, Smith reportedly was visited by the angel Moroni. Moroni said that he had come directly from the presence of God, and that God had chosen young Smith to restore the true Christian church, whose doctrines had been corrupted over the centuries.

You may know the rest of the story. The angel directed young Joseph to a nearby hillside where Joseph allegedly dug up some ancient tablets covered with hieroglyphics. Smith carried the plates home, and, even though he knew only English, he began translating them. He worked for days on end, stopping only for short breaks to eat or sleep. Finally, when the monumental task was completed, Moroni supposedly appeared again and took the strange tablets back to heaven.

Today, we all know Joseph Smith as the founder of the Mormon religion, and the work he "translated" as the *Book of Mormon.*

But there are some things about Joseph Smith you may not know. For instance, before his encounter with the angel, young Smith allegedly had been involved in the occult. In fact, he had developed something of a reputation as a "seer."

On May 3, 1877, an article in the *Chenengo Union* newspaper of Norwich, New York, reported:

> In the year 1825, we often saw in that quiet hamlet Joseph Smith Jr. . . . (living with) the family of Deacon Isaiah Stowell . . . (who had) a monomaniacal impression to seek for hidden treasures, which he believed were hidden in the earth. . . .
>
> Mr. Stowell . . . heard of the fame of . . . Joseph,

who by the aid of a magic stone had become a famous seer of lost or hidden treasures. . . . He with the magic stone was at once transferred from his humble abode to the more pretentious mansion of Deacon Stowell.

Here, in the estimation of the deacon, he confirmed his conceded powers as a seer, by means of the stone, which he placed in his hat. And by excluding the light from all other terrestrial things could see whatever he wished, even in the depths of the earth.

This poses an interesting question: Did Joseph Smith's venture into the occult pave the way for his encounter with the "angel" Moroni? Certainly the theology of the Mormon Church contains many elements found throughout occult literature.

Mormons, for example, believe that the God who rules over the earth is not Lord over the rest of the universe. They believe there are many planets with intelligent life on them, and that each of these planets is subject to a different god. In fact, they believe that all human beings have within them the potential to be like God.

Sound familiar?

Islam and Mormonism are two vastly different religions whose founders said they were influenced and guided by angels. Their teachings don't agree with each other, nor do they agree with all the basic tenets of Christianity.

WHOM DO YOU TRUST?

This leads us to a vital question: How can we tell God's side from the dark side in what we read about angels? Or, if an angel appears to us, how do we know we can trust him? Here are the facts, according to the Bible:

- Any angel who directs our attention to himself or who lets us worship him shouldn't be listened to. Angels who come from heaven always seek to direct attention and worship to God.
- An angel who tells us that we have the power within us to bring about our own salvation or to accomplish other great things isn't to be trusted. Angels who come from God understand that we are all powerless apart from Him, and that it is only through His power that we are able to do anything at all.
- If an angelic visitor tells us *anything* that contradicts the Bible in any way, we can be sure he doesn't have our best intentions at heart. But then again, we have to know the Bible if we're going to catch those contradictions! So we must study the Word. It is our best protection against false doctrine.

TOP TEN LIES ABOUT ANGELS

Phillips lists several lies about angels often contained in literature on the occult.[3] They are:

1. We should seek angels.

Many of today's most popular "experts" on angels teach that we should seek to have experiences with angels. They offer ways to help make these experiences possible, including:

- Meditation
- The chanting of mantras
- Summoning the angels by name

Let's look briefly at each of these practices.

First, meditation. There is a huge difference between biblical meditation and meditation as it is taught by today's New Age teachers. Biblical meditation involves contemplation of Scripture and *filling* our mind with God's majesty. Occultic meditation involves *emptying* our mind in order to encounter supernatural creatures or experiences.

Next, the chanting of mantras. A mantra is a word repeated again and again in order to relax the body and enter an altered state of consciousness. Again, it involves emptying the mind and thereby opens us up to dangerous supernatural influences.

Then, the naming of angels. In her book *Angels of Mercy*, Rosemary Ellen Guiley writes,

> We must discover names for our guardian angels if we wish them to manifest in their fullest magnitude. Name is an important ritual: it defines and it invests life, power, and potential. Without names, we cannot call out to the higher planes; we cannot invoke or evoke the beings, forces, and energies into our own dimension.[4]

It's very interesting to me that demonic rituals also call for the summoning of demons by name. I can't help but wonder who is really being summoned here.

The truth is that there is no legitimate power in the names of angels, but only in the name of Jesus. And the Bible says that we are to seek after God alone. The person who is chasing after encounters with angels has been distracted from the only thing that is of lasting importance—a relationship with God.

As I said in my FORBIDDEN DOORS series:

> Angels, heaven, hell, the supernatural—all are legitimate experiences if they come from God. But when we take a shortcut and try to create a supernatural experience on our own—through meditation, channeling, Ouija boards, drugs, crystals—we open ourselves up to possible satanic counterfeit.[5]

2. Angels work miracles.

In *The Angel Book*, Karen Goldman says that "the angel in you can heal you in many ways. Angels can help to heal illness, poverty, anger, despair. There is an abundance of pure healing energy, joy, creativity, and unwavering inner strength available for you at all times."[6]

Where is there room for God in all of this? Angels aren't in the miracle-making business. Miracles—including healing—are God's line of work.

3. All angels tell the truth.

We've already seen that this isn't the case. Angels aren't infallible beings. Remember that Satan himself was once a high-ranking angel, presumably an archangel, and yet Jesus said of him: "He was a murderer from the beginning, not holding to the truth, for there is no truth in him. When he lies, he speaks his native language, for he is a liar and the father of lies" (John 8:44).

4. When you are lost, angels desire to get "right inside your heart" and lead you home.

This is highly dangerous. *Demons* desire to get inside of you, and when they do it's called "possession." Anyone who invites an angel into his heart in this way opens himself up to demonic control. The Bible tells us that it is the Holy Spirit's job to lead and guide us from within—and His job alone.

5. Angels can help us gain access to heaven.

According to Jesus, "I am the way and the truth and the life. No one comes to the Father except through me" (John 14:6). The only way we can get to heaven is to surrender our life to Christ, accept the fact that He paid the price for our sins when He was crucified, and believe that He was resurrected on the third day.

6. Human beings are able to become angels.

The Bible says we and angels are two distinct creations. We are not angels, nor will we ever be. In fact, Scripture says you and I will one day judge the angels (see 1 Cor. 6:3).

7. Angels serve only to uncover our innate goodness and divinity.

The Bible doesn't teach that we have innate goodness or divinity. Instead, we are a fallen race, tainted by the sin of the first man. The Bible says that "all have sinned and fall short of the glory of God" (Rom. 3:23).

8. Angels are always trying to reach out to us.

The truth is that real angels reach out to us only when God commands them to do so. They are His messengers, His servants, and their desire is to do His will, period.

9. Angels can be felt in every atom of creation.

No way! As Phillips writes, "It is God who indwells every atom of creation by virtue of His creative power."[7]

10. Angels know what it is like to be you.

While it is true that angels are created beings just as you and I are, they don't know what it is like to be human. They will never know the joy of salvation. Jesus Christ died for the sins of humankind, but not to redeem angels. Angels know and love God deeply, but they can never sing "Amazing Grace" the way we can!

THEN WHAT DO ANGELS DO?

I've spent so much time talking about what angels don't do that you might think my intent is to disregard the importance of angels in general. Not at all. Angels are vital beings in God's kingdom. They are His ministering servants. The Bible tells us that they worship before His throne in heaven, having direct access to His presence. They are His messengers. They are His warriors, doing battle against the armies of Satan. At God's command, they watch over us and protect us.

The Bible tells us that when Jesus returns to earth, He will come "in his glory and in the glory of the Father and of the holy angels" (Luke 9:26). Jesus also said, "Whoever acknowledges me before men, the Son of Man will also acknowledge him before the angels of God. But he who disowns me before men will be disowned before the angels of God" (Luke 12:8–9). Obviously, then, angels are key creatures in God's design of the universe.

My quarrel here is not with angels—I wouldn't dare quarrel with angels!—but with beings who claim to be angels and are not, and with angels who claim to speak for God, but who in reality lost that right countless years ago!

The Bible tells us to "test the spirits" in order to be certain that they come from God (see 1 John 4:1–3). Certainly God also expects us to "test the angels."

I do believe that God's angels are watching over us every minute of the day, doing their best to keep us from harm. But I also believe they reveal their true identity to us only when it is absolutely necessary for them to do so. Most of the time they stay in the background, silent and invisible.

Other times we may encounter them and not even know that we were in their presence.

That's why the book of Hebrews says, "Do not forget to entertain strangers, for by so doing some people have entertained angels without knowing it" (13:2).

IN SUMMARY

God's angels

- are His warriors and His messengers, and as such, they will never tell you anything that is contrary to His Word as contained in the Bible;
- are never willing to accept the praise or worship of human beings;
- always seek to bring glory to God and His Son, Jesus Christ;
- rejoice whenever a sinner comes into God's kingdom through the only means possible—faith in Christ;
- understand that we are all powerless apart from God;
- are ministering spirits who walk alongside the faithful, ministering to and encouraging those who strive to live for God;
- come to us to lead us to God.

Satan's angels

- are his warriors and his messengers, and as such they often claim to be bringing "new and better truths" to

replace or update what is contained in the Bible;
- readily accept and even invite human praise and worship;
- deny or downplay Christ's divinity;
- say that there are many paths to peace with God;
- tell us that we have the power within us to become like God;
- are anxious to "get inside us," to take control;
- come to us to lead us away from God.

One final note. When people of the Bible encountered angels, they were struck with terror and fear. When practitioners of the occult meet their angels, they are often filled with warm fuzzies. What's the mix-up?

Next, we're going to take a look at some supernatural beings just about everybody's afraid of . . . and with good reason.

Held Hostage by the Devil

Are demons real?

You bet they are.

Who are they?

Most believe demons are evil angels intent on tormenting the human race.

As we discussed in the last chapter, evidence indicates that demons, in fact, started out in heaven just like all the other angels, but were cast out when they aligned themselves with Satan in his attempt to wrest control of the universe from God. Over the centuries, these creatures haven't done much to improve themselves. In fact, if anything, they seem to have grown even more corrupt and evil. If there was ever a single spark of goodness in them, it burned itself out long ago.

Demons will spend eternity in hell, and their one pleasure in life seems to be taking as many human souls with them as they possibly can. Demons hate God. They hate me. And they hate you. They enjoying seeing us suffer and they will do everything they possibly can to hurt us. Why? The best way to hurt God is to hurt His kids.

Sometimes demons decide that the best way to hurt us is to come to us on angels' wings, speaking of love, peace, and brotherhood, believing that to be the best means of enticing us away from God. Later, when they know they have the upper hand in someone's life, they come in with fangs bared, snarling and growling like the monsters they are. Other times they are more subtle, content to work through drugs, alcohol, pornography, and other such vices, never giving a hint that anything supernatural is going on until it's too late.

YOU HAVE NOTHING TO FEAR

Before we get further into our discussion of demons, there is one vital point we need to remember:

If you have given your life to Christ, you have absolutely nothing to fear from demons.

In fact, if you're a Christian, demons are afraid of you! Why? Because they know God has given you authority over them. Jesus says of those who belong to Him, "In my name they will drive out demons" (Mark 16:17).

If you are a believer, you have the right to act in the authority of Christ, and demons have no choice but to obey you.

Yes, demons are scary. They may threaten, pull off some spine-tingling parlor tricks, or rattle a few chains, but if your faith is in Jesus Christ instead of their lies and special effects, they have no choice but to flee when you confront them—like cockroaches that run for cover when the light is switched on!

On the other hand, please remember that the name of Jesus in itself isn't a magic wand that anybody can use to take authority over a demon. If you aren't living for Christ, you have no right to use His name or His authority. It's only when you are in right relationship with Him that you can fight demons and win!

Otherwise, you might find yourself in the same embarrassing situation as befell the seven sons of Sceva:

> Some Jews who went around driving out evil spirits tried to invoke the name of the Lord Jesus over those who were demon-possessed. They would say, "In the name of Jesus, whom Paul preaches, I command you to come out." Seven sons of Sceva, a Jewish chief priest, were doing this. One day the evil spirit answered them, "Jesus I know, and I know about Paul, but who are you?" Then the man who had the evil spirit jumped on them and overpowered them all. He gave them such a beating that they ran out of the house naked and bleeding. (Acts 19:13–16)

The sons of Sceva believed there was power in the name of Jesus, and they were right. The problem occurred when they thought anybody had the right to use the power of His name.

That's just one of the mistakes people make when it comes to dealing with demons. Here are some others.

FALSE BELIEF #1: DEMONS AREN'T REAL

Many "educated" people reject belief in demons as a relic of a superstitious age.

But Jesus Christ himself testifies to their existence.

In fact, during His earthly ministry, Jesus had many encounters with them. If Jesus believes in demons, that's enough reason for us to believe in them, too.

And what is Jesus' attitude about demons? He sees them as our enemy, and He comes against them at every opportunity. Read through the New Testament and you'll find several accounts like this one:

> Just then a man in their synagogue who was possessed by an evil spirit cried out, "What do you want with us, Jesus of Nazareth? Have you come to destroy us? I know who you are—the Holy One of God!"
>
> "Be quiet!" said Jesus sternly. "Come out of him!" The evil spirit shook the man violently and came out of him with a shriek. (Mark 1:23–25)

The fifth chapter of Mark tells of a man who was inhabited by many demons. The Bible says that this man "lived in the tombs, and no one could bind him any more, not even with a chain. For he had often been chained hand and foot, but he tore the chains apart and broke the irons on his feet. No one was strong enough to subdue him. Night and day among the tombs and in the hills he would cry out and cut himself with stones" (5:3–5).

When Jesus cast the demons out of the man, they went into a herd of pigs feeding nearby, and "The herd, about two thousand in number, rushed down the steep bank into the lake and were drowned." After that, the people of the area were afraid, and begged Jesus to leave when "they saw the man who had been possessed by the legion of demons, sitting there, dressed and in his right mind" (vv. 13–15).

Again and again as we read through the Gospels, we find that Jesus had absolute authority over demons. There was never an instance where they could withstand His power for even a second.

The ninth chapter of Mark tells of a time when a worried father brought his demon-possessed son to Jesus' apostles for help and they were unable to give it. But when Jesus arrived on the scene and commanded the demon to leave the child alone, "the spirit shrieked, convulsed him violently and came out. The boy looked so much like a corpse that many said, 'He's dead.' But Jesus took him by the hand and lifted him to his feet, and he stood up" (vv. 26–27).

The Bible goes on to say that "after Jesus had gone indoors, his disciples asked him privately, 'Why couldn't we drive it out?' He replied, 'This kind can come out only by prayer' " (vv. 28–29).

We can see from these passages of Scripture and many others that demons were very real and very active in the days when Jesus walked this earth in the flesh. And they are every bit as real and active today.

FALSE BELIEF #2: DEMONS ARE NEUTRAL

Some people believe demons really aren't so bad. In fact, they say, demons are really good guys who harass us to help us grow and mature. Like tough drill sergeants, they curse, swear, and threaten us only because they want to see us become all we can be.

Demons, they say, mean us no harm. They are simply the yin to God's yang. (Or is it the yang to His yin?)

John Randolph Price, in his book *The Angels Within Us—A Spiritual Guide to the Twenty-Two Angels That Govern Our Lives*, says of demons:

> I prefer to think of them as angels of light—whether from earth or other worlds. They search, select, and guide those men and women who may be suitable subjects . . . a Master may then instruct, or plant the seed of a new concept . . . and the word is spread, taking hold and growing in the mind of others, until there is a wave of collective thinking sufficiently powerful to change events and shape the future.[1]

In a nutshell, he's stating that demons can be our allies.

But the truth is that demons aren't our helpers. They want to destroy us—mind, body, and spirit—and they go to great lengths to get what they want.

Still, New Age author David Spangler even has good words for the devil himself—Lucifer, the prince of demons. Spangler writes that "Christ is the same force as Lucifer."[2] He also says that "Lucifer works within each of us to bring us to wholeness as we move into the New Age," adding that "Lucifer comes to give us the final gift of wholeness. If we accept it, then he is free and we are free."[3]

Radio personality Benjamin Creme took Spangler's teaching one step further when he told an international audience that Lucifer was "the sacrificial lamb" who paid the supreme sacrifice for our planet. Once again, Satan is attempting to usurp Christ's position.

FALSE BELIEF #3: DEMONS ARE EVERYWHERE

Earlier I quoted C. S. Lewis, who said there are two equally dangerous extremes when it comes to thinking about demons. The first is to disbelieve in them—to ignore them. The second is to give them too much credit—to think about them too much.

In the not-too-distant past, some Christians put far too much emphasis on demons. It got to the point where one guy who was having car trouble asked me to help him cast the demons out of his engine. I had to pass. I figured a 30,000-mile tune-up would do a lot more for that car than an exorcism.

During that time some people taught that we all had been invaded by demons, and there were gatherings where paper bags were handed out so people could vomit up the demons that were tormenting them. It was all pretty weird. And unhealthy. And unnecessary.

Now the pendulum may have swung back too far in the other direction.

Back then demons were blamed for all sorts of things they weren't responsible for.

But today many believe evil is solely the result of man's fallen nature.

It's true that human beings don't always need demons to inspire them to new heights of evil. As Jesus said, "Out of the heart come evil thoughts, murder, adultery, sexual immorality, theft, false testimony, slander" (Matt. 15:19).

It's easy for a person to point his finger and say, "The devil made me do it," when he's really just been following the worst instincts of his own heart.

On the other hand, demons are real. And they stop at nothing in their attempt to get us to cheat, lie, steal, kill, commit adultery, do anything contrary to God's law. They love it when we hurt other people. They love it when we hurt ourselves. And most of all, they love it when we grieve God.

HOW DEMONS OPERATE

Most of the time demons aren't able to exert direct control over us. Instead, they use guerrilla warfare, zinging us as often as they can from the outside. They put various types of temptation in front of us. (Remember the Lord's Prayer? "Lead us not into temptation, but deliver us from evil.") They hit us with impure thoughts. They try to get us to doubt God and distrust His Word. They tempt us to exercise the worst of our flesh—anger, selfishness, lust, violence, and cruelty.

But demons aren't content to direct things from the sidelines. They want to dive into the middle of the action. If they can find a way, they get inside a person and rule his life completely. This is demonic possession.

It's real and it happens, as the Bible and numerous missionaries can attest.

CHATTING WITH DEMONS

What do you think of when you hear the word "demons"?

If you're a fan of late-night television, you probably think of Linda Blair, who starred as the demon-possessed teenager in the 1970s movie *The Exorcist.*

You may remember Ms. Blair sitting in bed with her head spinning around or engaging in some very nasty projectile vomiting.

The Exorcist—which was supposedly based (loosely) on

49

a real-life case of demon possession that had been investigated by the Roman Catholic Church—was a blockbuster movie that got the whole world talking about demons.

I didn't need *The Exorcist* to convince me of the reality of demons. It was while that movie was still popular that I had my own encounter with them.

Oh, I considered seeing the movie . . . to find out what all the fuss was about. In fact, I was on my way to see it one night when I suddenly began to sense that God didn't want me to go—that He didn't want me to see any film that glorified demonic power. As a result, I was probably one of the few people in the entire world who missed Linda Blair's gross-out performance.

But it was God's grace that prevented me from seeing *The Exorcist.* Otherwise I might have been ready to run the other way when a few months later I received a telephone call from the man I mentioned in the last chapter who spoke to "angels." Let's call him Jerry. As I mentioned, I eventually realized something was fishy about his "angels." One of the clues was his continual begging them not to hurt me. For heavenly creatures, they didn't seem all that loving.

Another thing that bothered me was how Jerry said he always felt sick to his stomach right before one of the "angels" took over and spoke through him. As I mentioned before, Jerry had received some public acclaim from the powers these entities gave him, and he was quite proud of that—but whatever was happening to him, the experience was far from pleasant.

It took a while, but I eventually worked up the courage to ask one of Jerry's mysterious friends that all-important question: "Is Jesus Christ your Lord?"

When the answer came, "Not only is He my Lord . . . He's also my brother," I knew Jerry was in trouble. I didn't understand a whole lot about demons at the time, but I knew enough to know that any time you come into contact with an entity that claims equality with Christ, you aren't dealing with the good guys.

I wasn't sure how to handle the situation, never having come face-to-face—or even telephone-to-telephone—with a demon. But I did tell Jerry that he really was in contact with demons, not angels. He reacted just as I feared. He insisted I was wrong and worried that if I pushed the issue he might lose his powers. I pleaded with him to give me his address so I could come visit him in person and pray for him, but he was too frightened.

Soon a tug-of-war raged inside Jerry. One minute I was talking to Jerry . . . the next, one of the entities . . . and then Jerry again. When the "angels" had control of Jerry, they insulted me and called me foul names. When Jerry was in control, he kept begging his angels not to hurt me. Finally, twenty-four hours later, after he had called dozens of times, he gasped out his address.

The next day I went to see Jerry, accompanied by a friend from my church. Before we went, we bowed our heads in my car and confessed all our sins to God, asking for forgiveness in the name of Christ. We knew that we had better be in proper relationship with God when we walked into Jerry's house. We didn't want to give the devil any ammunition to use against us.

I admit that my heart was pounding in my chest when we walked up the short sidewalk to Jerry's place. I wasn't comforted by the fact that he lived in a neatly kept house in a suburban neighborhood. It didn't exactly look like the sort of place where demons hung out. Still, I was worried about the battle that awaited us.

However, the moment Jerry opened the door, every ounce of fear vanished. He stood before me, a short, balding, fiftyish gentleman full of fear—a man who desperately wanted to be right with God. The moment I saw him, I was filled with such love that I instinctively threw my arms around him and hugged him.

It was the right thing to do. Later on he told me that at that moment he realized he could trust me completely.

We went into Jerry's living room, sat down, chitchatted for a while, and finally began to pray with him. As we did, Jerry started to writhe and scream—although I knew it wasn't really Jerry.

When we sang worship songs, he really seemed to be in agony. The more worshipful the song, the louder he screamed and the more his body jerked and contorted.

After a while, when our prayers seemed to be losing steam, I decided to recite the Lord's Prayer. That really sent Jerry into a frenzy. He howled as if I was pouring acid on him.

At first I didn't understand what was going on. What was so different about the Lord's Prayer that it would cause these entities to react in this way? Then it dawned on me. I was praying the Word of God! This was the weapon Jesus himself had used to fight Satan when they battled on the Mount of Temptation!

No wonder the Bible tells us that the Word of God is sharper than a two-edged sword!

I pulled out my Bible, turned to the Psalms, and began to read. The reaction was immediate and severe. Screaming. Swearing. Howling. Gnashing of teeth.

Finally, my friend and I got down on our knees in front of Jerry, laid hands on him, and began to pray for his deliverance. The first two or three demons surfaced and were easily disposed of in Jesus' name. But others were more deeply entrenched in Jerry's life. Some had been with him since he was a small child, and they did not want to let go. We prayed and prayed and prayed some more, but these stronger demons made it clear they were not leaving without a fight.

Now, as I said, my friend and I had never encountered demons before and were a little unsure of the procedure. We didn't want the demons to hurt Jerry by throwing him on the ground, so we held him down pretty good while we prayed for him. It was during this time that another fellow came walking through the front door—Jerry's roommate. I'm sure we made quite a scene. For all he knew, we were a couple of burglars who'd been caught in the act. He could have ordered us to leave his friend alone. He could have threatened to call the police.

Instead, all he said was "Hi, guys." He acted as if it were the most natural thing in the world to see two big men holding little Jerry down like that. He went on into the kitchen, made himself a sandwich, and then left again.

Later on Jerry asked him why he didn't try to stop us or at least ask us what we were doing.

"It was the oddest sensation," the man replied. "But there was something different about those guys. Were they . . . angels?"

"Angels . . . no . . . why?"

"I'm not really sure. I just knew I wasn't supposed to try to stop them."

Well, our session with Jerry went on for hours, as various demons were brought to the surface and cast out in Jesus' name. It was interesting that each had its own particular character trait. For example, one of them had very strong homosexual tendencies. He called himself "the Persian boy" and claimed to be a departed spirit who had once had a homosexual relationship with either Napoleon or Alexander the Great. He spoke in a male voice, but with exaggerated effeminate characteristics. While this demon was in control of him, Jerry's body language changed completely. He crossed his legs in a feminine manner, spoke with a lisp, and seemed to be a completely different person. But as soon as we had taken authority over the demon and removed him in Christ's name, Jerry was back to his old self.

Now, before I go on, I want to make it clear that I don't believe all homosexuality is caused by demons. I do believe that some demons may manifest homosexual behavior or tempt their victims with this particular sin. Demons show their presence in a variety of ways. The Bible tells us that Jesus cast out demons that caused their victims to be deaf and mute. Does this mean that all people who are deaf or who cannot speak are inhabited by demons? Of course not. But I believe there are demons that can render their victims deaf or mute.

The same can be said of people who are suffering from Multiple Personality Disorder. This is a legitimate psychological problem often brought about by severe trauma during childhood. People who suffer from it develop numerous distinct personalities in order to cope. Unfortunately, many well-meaning Christians have done more damage than good by mistaking this disorder for demonic activity and trying to "cast the demons out." This is why prayer for discernment is so vital in these situations.

Because of their supernatural insight, I was totally convinced that we weren't dealing with some type of psychological disorder, but rather with separate demonic entities who had invaded Jerry's life.

It was late in the evening by the time we finished ministering to him. It had been a long day, and we were exhausted. By our best count, we had successfully encountered and removed twelve of the creatures, and as far as I could tell, our time with Jerry had been a complete success. He seemed happy and relaxed and told us he couldn't remember when he had felt so peaceful.

But it didn't last. . . .

My wife and I were getting ready to go out for dinner the next night when the phone rang.

"Bill?" Jerry sounded frightened. "There's still some here."

He was agitated, and wanted me to come right away. But I had promised my wife a relaxed evening in a restaurant and I wasn't about to break that promise. I told him I'd come the following afternoon.

Immediately, a haughty, sarcastic voice took over.

"We won't be here," it told me. "We're taking him to New York, and there's not a thing you can do about it!"

"No way!" I said. "You're not going to do that. By the power and authority of Jesus Christ, you cannot take Jerry off that property until three o'clock tomorrow afternoon."

Then I hung up, and we went on to dinner.

The next day, my friend and I went back to Jerry's, and when we pulled up in front of his house, we were greeted by a strange sight. Jerry was pacing back and forth in his yard, looking much like a caged animal. Every once in a while, he tried to step onto the sidewalk, but he couldn't do it. He'd lift his leg in the air and lean forward, but there seemed to be an invisible barrier stopping him.

"Bill!" he yelled. "I don't know what's going on here . . . but I can't leave my yard!"

He didn't know what was going on, but I did. It was not

yet three o'clock. He couldn't leave his property until we got there to help him. It was at that moment, more than ever, that I was struck by the absolute authority that belongs to those who believe in Christ.

We took Jerry to our church office, where we were joined by some reinforcements, including singer Keith Green, who was an active member of the church. There were several more demons lurking down in Jerry's soul, including one that tried to get him to jump from an upstairs window.

As evening approached, I was completely drained. I just wanted to go home and sleep. Two days of intense battle with demons had taken its toll. I was more than a little relieved when it appeared that we were down to the last demon. But that last one was holding on with both claws, and it was not going to leave without putting up a fight.

Suddenly, one of our pastors—a man who was reluctant to believe in much of the supernatural—had a mental picture of Jesus standing off to the side, watching the proceedings. He told us later that he was watching as Jesus slowly turned and glanced in Jerry's direction.

None of the rest of us saw this. What we did see at that same moment was Jerry opening his mouth and letting out a shrill, bloodcurdling scream, unlike anything I have ever heard. By the time the scream had finished echoing up and down the halls of the church, the final demon was gone and Jerry was free at last.

When our friend told us about his vision of Jesus, I shook my head in awe. Our Lord didn't even have to speak a word to defeat the demon. A single glance was all it took.

I've heard some people say that God and Satan are adversaries. Equal but opposite forces. No way! If I didn't know it before, I learned that day that Satan is no adversary for God. He's nothing more than so much plaque on God's teeth!

If the subject of demons is new to you, you may be startled by the story I've just told. And you may ask some of the following questions.

What exactly is demonic possession?

Possession is what happens when a demon or demons actually take up residence inside a human body. As I mentioned before, demons are not content to merely harass us from the sidelines. If a demon sees a chance to enter into a man or woman's soul and take control, he will do it.

Why do they want to do this? It appears there are at least three reasons: First, it enables them to destroy a human being, and there's nothing they enjoy more.

Second, demons like to have a human body because it gives them a vehicle to carry out their diabolical plans. (Yes, I know "diabolical plans" sounds like something out of a mad-scientist movie, but there's nobody more diabolical than a demon.)

Third, demons attempt to possess us because they enjoy the pleasures of the flesh. They have insatiable appetites for things like illicit and perverted sex, alcohol, narcotics, and gambling. As a result, they often steer their victims into addictions in these areas.

How does possession happen?

Some people actually invite demons into their lives—a few because they believe they're opening themselves up to angels or, as is more commonly the case, spirit guides. Also, those who are deeply involved in occult practices are putting themselves into greater danger of demonic possession. The same goes for those who are involved in drugs. In Deuteronomy 18:10, the Bible warns that God's anger will fall upon those who "practice sorcery." The Greek root word for "sorcery" is *pharmakeia*, which means "drugs." It's the root from which we get our modern words "pharmacy" and "pharmaceuticals." It's not a coincidence that the Bible equates the use of narcotics with sorcery. There are documented cases of excessive use of addictive drugs leading to demonic enslavement.

Michael Fishback is the executive director of a rescue mission in San Bernardino, California. He's been working with the poor and homeless for more than two decades. He'll tell you that when he started out he didn't think much about demons. Like many Christians, he knew demons existed because the Bible talks about them, but he didn't think they were a real problem in today's world. Now he knows differently.

"I've seen so many things that can't be explained any other way," he says. "I've seen people that we could not help—at all—until we took authority in Jesus' name over the demonic influences in their lives."

Michael Fishback doesn't think all alcoholics or drug addicts are afflicted by demons. But he believes that some are, and these cannot be rehabilitated until they have been set free from demonic bondage. Again, discernment is the key. It's important that we *not* look at every evil habit or practice as a case of demonic oppression or possession. Some of it is just plain old-fashioned sin. So how can we tell?

How can we recognize possession?

It's not always easy to tell whether a person is demonized or suffering from some psychological ill. Is that guy controlled by demons, or is he suffering from schizophrenia? Is this woman a demoniac, or does she suffer from Multiple Personality Disorder? If we are confronted with a situation where we suspect demonic involvement but aren't sure, the best thing we can do is ask God to reveal the truth to us. And He will. Because if there is one Person even more concerned than we are about seeing demons' victims set free, it is our loving heavenly Father.

There is, however, one other surefire way I believe we can tell we are dealing with demons: As my experience with Jerry indicates, a person who is demonized cannot stand to listen to the Word of God or be in the presence of those who are worshiping the Lord.

Who has the authority to cast demons out of someone?

Anyone who has accepted Jesus Christ as his personal Savior and who is living in proper relationship with Him has the power and the authority to cast out demons in His name.

Having said that, I need to caution that going up against demons isn't easy and must not be taken lightly. If you aren't sure you're in right relationship with God, or if you have unconfessed sin in your life—take care of it first! Demons know what scares us and they use it. They know our weak spots and they hammer at them. They taunt us and laugh at us and ask us who we think we are that we can possibly defeat them, even though they know well that Christ has given us the power to do just that. I wouldn't recommend that anyone who is timid or squeamish get involved in a ministry of deliverance. And if you are a new Christian, never attempt to confront a demon unless you are accompanied by someone more mature in the faith.

How can you prevent possession?

The sure way to keep demons out of our life is not to open the door. Avoid practicing any type of occult activity. And stay close to God. As the Bible says, "Submit yourselves, then, to God. Resist the devil, and he will flee from you. Come near to God and he will come near to you" (James 4:7–8).

Demons can't stand to be in the presence of God. It follows, then, that if God is present in your life, demons won't want to be around you.

If God is at home in your life, it's the last place any demon will want to be.

Deliverance Isn't Enough

Before we leave the topic of demons behind, I want to make one thing very clear. When a person is inhabited by demons, it's not enough to cast them out in Jesus' name. Unless that person begins living for God and learns how to resist the devil's temptations, demons will return at their first opportunity.

Jesus put it this way:

> "When an evil spirit comes out of a man, it goes through arid places seeking rest and does not find it. Then it says, 'I will return to the house I left.' When it arrives, it finds the house swept clean and put in order. Then it goes and takes seven other spirits more wicked than itself, and they go in and live there. And the final condition of that man is worse than the first" (Luke 11:24–26).

Despite the great, dramatic conclusion of a successful deliverance, it's vital to understand that the battle isn't over. In her excellent book *Enticed by the Light*, Sharon Beekman explains how demons usually return to tempt and torment their ex-hosts over the next several months to years. We must stand beside a newly delivered believer, encouraging him or her not to give in to old patterns and to continually take authority over the voices until gradually they quit returning and trying to reenter.

Let me repeat: A successful deliverance is only the beginning of setting the new believer free.

There is much more we could say about demons. We could give example after example of their altogether evil nature and their determination to destroy anyone who comes in contact with them.

But the most important thing to know about demons is that they are absolutely powerless when confronted with the love and power of Jesus Christ. As long as we are in right relationship with Him, we have nothing at all to fear from the hosts of hell.

4

In League With the Devil

Look deep into the eyes of Sean Sellers and tell me what you see.

A "normal" young man. The boy next door. Perhaps a surfer or the best skateboarder in the neighborhood.

Certainly not a cold-blooded killer.

And yet in the middle of a quiet, ordinary night, Sean Sellers crept into the bedroom where his parents were sleeping and brutally murdered them.

He didn't do it because his parents were abusive—they weren't. Nor was it because there was friction in the family.

He did it because he believed it would bring him honor and power from his master.

Several weeks prior to the murder of his parents and the fatal shooting of a convenience store clerk earlier that same evening, Sean Sellers had dedicated his life to Satan.

Turn your attention for a moment to America's heartland—the city of Keokuk, Iowa. No one would expect to find devil worship in this all-American community. That's why residents here were shocked when two young men tried to kill themselves as a result of their involvement in satanism. One young man died. The other survived.

Pearl, Mississippi, also made headlines when a teenager there was arrested for killing his mother and a classmate, allegedly as the result of his involvement in a satanic group. He says now that the leaders of the group ordered him to carry out the killings and he obeyed. People were left shaking their heads and saying, "This kind of thing can't happen here." But it did.

What's going on? Why would anyone want to follow Satan down a road that leads to hell?

As we search for the answers, let's travel to upstate New York to visit a friend of mine—a fellow named David Berkowitz.

A REAL NICE GUY DOING "LIFE WITHOUT PAROLE"

David makes you feel at ease from the moment you meet him. He's a likable kind of guy with a twinkle in his eye.

In fact, the first time I met him I was tempted to ask him, "What's a nice guy like you doing in a place like this?"

You see, David Berkowitz is in prison. And he will stay there for the rest of his life. He's considered such a threat to society that when they locked him up, they threw away the key. Why? For a brief period in the mid-1970s, David Berkowitz terrorized New York City as the infamous "Son of Sam." That's how he signed letters to the New York City Police Department, in which he taunted them and vowed to continue a bloody killing spree that was making newspaper headlines across America. Before he was apprehended, Berkowitz was accused of shooting thirteen people, seven of whom died. When he was finally caught and convicted, his sentence was "life without possibility of parole."

Shortly after Berkowitz was arrested, he confessed to the killings but said that he had been commanded to kill by a neighbor's dog—named Sam. That was why he had referred to himself as "The Son of Sam."

As you can imagine, Berkowitz was written off as just another lunatic—a highly deadly lunatic—and locked up.

But today, more than twenty years after his arrest, Berkowitz says that there was never any dog named Sam. He concocted that story simply from fear of telling the truth. During the years since his arrest and conviction, though, David Berkowitz has seriously surrendered his life to Christ. And because he is a committed Christian, he wants to set the record straight regarding what really happened on the dark streets of New York City two decades ago.

He's not changing his story because he thinks it will help him. He believes he is serving a just sentence and knows that no matter what he does or says, he will never again be a free man. But he is serious about doing anything he can to help prevent others from throwing their lives away as he did.

Was there a Sam? Yes. But Sam wasn't an innocent neighborhood pooch. Sam was the nickname of a demon who had been summoned by the group of Satan worshipers to which Berkowitz belonged. It was the demon who ordered the murders, Berkowitz now says, and he obeyed—partly out of fear, partly out of peer pressure, and partly because he lacked the ability to disobey.

A FAMILIAR STORY

David Berkowitz had the personality profile of most of the young people who are attracted to Satan worship. Like Sean Sellers, he wasn't comfortable in school. He was bright, but his grades never reflected that intelligence. He didn't make friends easily and was something of a loner—an outcast.

David eventually dropped out of school, enlisted in the U.S. Army, and served a tour in Vietnam. He says that when he came home to New York, his dreams were the same as any other young man's. He wanted to find a nice girl, get married, settle down, and raise a family.

Instead, he found Satan.

David says that his descent into murderous madness began when he was "hanging out" and met some people who seemed to take an interest in him. He thought they were "cool." He was flattered by their interest. They had money to spend, and they liked having a good time.

These people accepted David, didn't judge him, and quickly won his friendship and loyalty. He had no idea that his new friends had sworn their allegiance to Satan. At first, they spoke of mysteries and secret ceremonies. He was intrigued.

Finally, he was invited to attend one of their gatherings. There it quickly became apparent what his new acquaintances were up to. They were deeply committed to the worship of Satan. David was repulsed, yes, but he was also fascinated and attracted. He should have run, but he didn't.

Over time he was drawn deeper and deeper into the satanic rituals. I don't believe it's necessary to discuss all of the things David participated in and experienced. Let me just say that according to what David told me, his acts grew more despicable and more violent.

Eventually the group summoned the demon who used David Berkowitz to feed his hunger for human misery. The members of the group called the demon "Sam," which was short for the name he gave them when he had first appeared.

Sam had stern words for Berkowitz and his fellow satanists. Satan wasn't satisfied with their puny sacrifices and empty talk about serving him. He wanted—no, commanded—them to prove their allegiance, and if they didn't obey there would be hell on earth to pay. He wanted the ultimate sacrifice—a human life.

David Berkowitz knew Sam meant business. If he disobeyed orders, whether from Sam or other members of the group, he or his family would be killed. And so, armed with his .44, David began prowling the streets of New York City, looking for victims. "The Son of Sam" became notorious from coast to coast, as the New York City Police Department tried desperately to find a way to prevent him from striking again.

Finally, police succeeded in capturing David. He was arrested and charged with seven counts of first-degree murder. The moment he was arrested, his friends disappeared. But he knew they were lurking nearby, and that if he implicated them in any way, they would kill him or his family.

He was tried, convicted, and sentenced. He never said a word about the other members of the group, some of whom, according to what David states now, had also been involved in the murders.

A NARROW ESCAPE FROM HELL

David Berkowitz probably would have been executed for his crimes had he not committed them during a time when the death penalty was banned in the United States. Today, he gives thanks for God's mercy, which spared his life. He knows that had he been executed, he would have gone straight to hell. But God had other plans for him, and it was in prison that he learned from a fellow inmate about the love of Christ. He renounced Satan, sought God's forgiveness for all the horrible things he had done, and became a Christian committed to serving others.

I admit that some people don't believe a word David Berkowitz says. They still write him off as a psychopath looking for a way to justify what he did. But I've spent hours talking with him. I've asked tough, skeptical questions, and I have come to believe him—not only because of his words but because of his deeds. Today, David Berkowitz leads Bible studies and prayer groups, works with mental patients, and raises money for overseas missions. One village in Africa has even named a child after him.

I've asked myself what reasons he could possibly have for inventing this story. He knows he's never going to get out of prison. He's certainly not trying to exonerate himself; he freely admits that he committed many of the murders and takes full responsibility for his actions. As far as I can tell, there is only one reason why he decided to speak about what really happened in New York all those years ago. He wants to tell all who will listen about the redeeming power of Jesus Christ and warn them about the dangers of satanism.

WHY WOULD ANYONE BECOME A SATANIST?

And yet despite warnings from people like David Berkowitz, many people in our society—especially the young— are attracted to Satan worship. They get involved with satanism for many reasons, but most of all because it gives them a sense of power or control.

As one teenager said, "The other kids know I'm into it and they treat me with respect." Like David Berkowitz, this young man has trouble fitting in. He feels like an outcast, and he is pushed around and picked on.

Some are attracted to the worship of Satan through the example of their heroes—especially heroes from the world of rock music. This is really nothing new. As early as the 1960s the Rolling Stones promoted their image as "the bad boys of rock 'n' roll" by giving two of their albums satanic titles: *Their Satanic Majesties' Request* and *Goat's Head Soup*.

I certainly don't believe that all rock musicians are sold out to the devil or that all rock music is dangerous. But I also think it's important to be wise when it comes to selecting the music we hear. Listening to lyrics full of reference to violence, illicit sex, despair, and death can't be healthy.

Researcher John Charles Cooper puts it this way:

> It is fanatical to believe that every youth who plays fantasy games or enjoys heavy metal rock music is into occultism, but young people found engaged in destructive occultism usually are involved in thrash metal. . . . The lyrics, dress, symbols, and lifestyles of these heavy metal singers and performers make satanism attractive to many young people from a very early age. Join the sadistic lyrics and blatantly perverse sexuality of these rock bands to the intoxication of pot, alcohol, or hard drugs, and you have very heavy conditioning that might well tip a teenager into antisocial behavior.[1]

As I've said, satanism in rock music is nothing new. Marilyn Manson, with his multi-platinum album *Antichrist Su-*

perstar, was just the latest in a long line of rock musicians who claimed or inferred some relationship to the devil. Some may be quite serious. Others present themselves as satanists merely because it makes them seem sinister and dangerous and, therefore, helps them sell more CDs.

According to Bob and Gretchen Passantino, noted experts on satanism:

> Even the most explicitly satanic band, Slayer, denies its members actually practice satanism or believe in the demonic supernatural their lyrics celebrate. King Diamond is the only widely popular metal musician to consider himself a serious, dedicated satanist, and Diamond carefully explains that he doesn't believe in the supernatural—only in natural forces beyond most humans' knowledge or control.[2]

The Passantinos also quote Diamond as saying:

> When I use the word Satan, it doesn't stand for a guy with horns. To me, that word means the powers of the unknown, the powers of darkness. . . . I don't believe in heaven, and I don't believe in hell as a place with flames where people are burning and having eternal pain. I don't believe in that at all. I believe in a place I call "beyond."[3]

Is King Diamond right? Are we merely living in a *Star Wars* type of universe, surrounded by "forces" we can use either for good or evil? Or are musicians like Diamond,

Slayer, and others playing with forces they don't understand—forces that will eventually turn against them and destroy them?

Bob and Gretchen Passantino and others answer that question by telling of several young people whose suicides were related, in some way, to heavy metal/satanic music.[4]

A RELIGION OF SELFISHNESS

I am convinced Satan also likes us to accept the lie that there is no such thing as a personal embodiment of evil. He doesn't care much whether or not we believe in him. He'd much rather have us disbelieve in God. He seems happy if he can get us to live in some moral never-never land where everything is relative, there's no such thing as absolute good or evil, and everyone is free to follow their own inclinations in every situation.

He claims that God is a killjoy who only wants to stifle us and keep us from realizing our full potential. "Enjoy life," he says. "Have fun. Don't limit yourself." But can you imagine living in a world where everyone did exactly as he pleased? It doesn't sound much like paradise to me. It's hard to comprehend the chaos that would result from such unbridled selfishness. And yet this is exactly the kind of world satanists strive for. "Do what you will" is the cornerstone statement upon which Satan has built his kingdom.

The Church of Satan, founded by Anton LaVey, is built upon selfishness and greed, as exemplified by the *Nine Satanic Statements* listed in the following chart.[5] I couldn't resist including nine rebuttal statements from the Bible:

1. Satan represents indulgence, instead of abstinence.

   1. "Offer your bodies as living sacrifices, holy and pleasing to God" (Rom. 12:1).

2. Satan represents vital existence, instead of spiritual pipe dreams.

   2. "I [Jesus] have come that they may have life, and have it to the full" (John 10:10).

3. Satan represents undefiled wisdom, instead of hypocritical self-deceit.

   3. "The fear of the Lord is the beginning of knowledge, but fools despise wisdom and discipline" (Prov. 1:7).

4. Satan represents kindness to those who deserve it, instead of love wasted on ingrates.

   4. "Love your enemies, do good to those who hate you, bless those who curse you, pray for those who mistreat you" (Luke 6:27–28).

5. Satan represents vengeance, instead of turning the other cheek.

   5. "If someone strikes you on one cheek, turn to him the other also" (Luke 6:29).

6. Satan represents responsibility to the responsible, instead of concern for psychic vampires.

   6. "Do good to all people" (Gal. 6:10).

7. Satan represents man as just another animal, sometimes better, more often worse than those that walk on all fours, who, because of his "divine spiritual and intellectual development," has become the most vicious of all.

   7. "God created man in his own image" (Gen. 1:27).

8. Satan represents all of the so-called sins, as they all lead to physical, mental, or emotional gratification.

8. "The wages of sin is death" (Rom. 6:23).

9. Satan has been the best friend the church has ever had, as he has kept it in business all these years.

9. "Your enemy the devil prowls around like a roaring lion looking for someone to devour. Resist him, standing firm in the faith" (1 Peter 5:8–9).

It's easy to see the differences in philosophy between those who follow Satan and those who belong to God. It's also easy to see the different societies such philosophies would ultimately produce. Here are a few other reasons why following Satan is a bad idea:

1. In the war for control of the universe, Satan has already been defeated.

Satan has kicked up quite a bit of dust over the centuries and caused a lot of trouble, but he has no chance at all of wresting control of the universe from God. Anyone who believes that Satan is ultimately going to emerge victorious operates under the false assumption that God and Satan are equals. This is far from the truth. Satan and God are opposites, in that God is pure goodness and Satan is pure evil—but they are not equals. Satan's opposite number would most likely be an archangel, such as Michael or Gabriel. Archangels are powerful, yes, but they are created beings just like you and me, and not God-like in any way, shape, or form.

It is a lie that Satan is the "dark lord" of the underworld, or that he is going to be some sort of supreme ruler in hell. I don't even know where we got that idea. It certainly isn't what the Bible teaches. Satan is going to wind up in hell, yes, but he's not going to be the all-powerful warden there. He is merely going to be an inmate.

Some religions teach that God and Satan have both existed forever, that they might be considered opposite sides of the same coin. Another falsehood. Satan is a created being, the work of God's hand. But like his human counterparts, he was given free will to choose whether he would do good or evil. He chose evil. His existence had a beginning and it will have an end. His fate is already sealed. The Bible explains: "And the devil . . . was thrown into the lake of burning sulfur . . . and . . . will be tormented day and night for ever and ever" (Rev. 20:10).

In short, that doesn't sound like the sort of general I'd want to follow into battle.

2. Satan always plays into God's hand.

Romans 8:28 assures us that "in all things God works for the good of those who love him, who have been called according to his purpose." That doesn't mean that Christians aren't going to go through trials and tribulations. All of us go through bad times. Jesus warned us it would be that way: "In this world you will have trouble. But take heart! I have overcome the world" (John 16:33).

What that passage in Romans means is that if we belong

to God, even when bad things happen to us we can rest in the knowledge that something good is going to come out of it. For the Christian, everything that happens to us ultimately benefits us in some way.

God is capable of taking everything Satan means for evil and turning it into good. In one sense, you can't help but feel a little sorry for Satan when you see how hard he works to defeat God, and yet how he plays into His hands at every turn.

Even when Satan thought he had won his greatest victory, it became his most devastating defeat. I am talking, of course, about the crucifixion of Christ. Satan thought he had won the war. He must have been beside himself with joy when he saw the Lord nailed to the cross. He must have been delighted as he watched the Son of God die slowly in agony and thrilled when he saw the spear thrust into Jesus' side, indicating that He was dead.

But what Satan didn't know was that it was all part of God's plan to liberate us from the bondage of sin. Satan had done exactly what God wanted him to do. And Satan's choke hold on this planet was completely broken when Jesus walked out of the tomb three days later.

Today, Satan is still defeated by God at every turn. I believe that God allows him to test and challenge us because it helps to keep us alert, on guard, and dedicated in our service to the Lord. Yes, I know the pain and suffering Satan causes is real, but if he wasn't always on the attack it would be fairly easy to become complacent and lethargic.

I'm reminded of a story I heard about attempts to ship fresh North Atlantic cod from Boston to San Francisco during the nineteenth century. At that time the only way to ship the fish to the West Coast was to sail around the South American continent—a trip that took months. As you can imagine, the first attempts to dress the cod in Boston and pack them in ice failed miserably. By the time they reached California, the fish weren't exactly fit for consumption.

Next, the cod were placed in holding tanks full of water, shipped to California alive, and dressed there. The results were less than satisfactory. The fish didn't get much exercise during the trip, and as a result they were pasty and relatively tasteless.

Finally, someone hit upon an interesting idea.

"Why don't we put some catfish in with the cod?" Why? Because catfish are cods' natural enemy. Sure enough, when a few catfish were placed in those tanks with them, the cod were always alert and swimming around. This time, when the fish reached San Francisco, they were in perfect shape.

You might say that Satan is nothing more than a catfish in the water to ensure that our spiritual muscles are kept firm and in good shape. Or as James 1:2–4 says:

> Consider it pure joy, my brothers, whenever you face trials of many kinds, because you know that the testing of your faith develops perseverance. Perseverance must finish its work so that you may be mature and complete, not lacking anything.

3. Satan wants to destroy everyone—including his own soldiers.

Where is David Berkowitz today? He's doing life in prison. Ditto Sean Sellers. It ought to be clear that Satan isn't the least bit interested in protecting his own. Satan isn't interested in helping anybody for any reason. Instead, he knows that he is eventually "going down," and he's determined to take as many of us with him as he possibly can. He promises rewards, but he never, ever delivers.

That's the way he's always been:

He promised Adam and Eve knowledge and wisdom if they would disobey God and eat the forbidden fruit. Instead, they received a death sentence.

Satan even tried to get Jesus to turn away from His mission by showing Him the great kingdoms of the world and promising, "I will give you all their authority and splendor, for it has been given to me, and I can give it to anyone I want to. So if you worship me, it will all be yours" (Luke 4:7). But Jesus saw through the scam and answered, "It is written: 'Worship the Lord your God and serve him only'" (Luke 4:8).

Satan tries to get people to obey him by making wild promises he'll never fulfill. But if he can't get people to obey him by sweet-talking them, he threatens them: "Obey me or I'll destroy you." David Berkowitz feared that if he didn't obey the will of Satan, he would be destroyed. He obeyed, and in many ways his life was destroyed anyway.

When it comes to a partnership with Satan, nobody wins.

4. Satan can't touch us if we belong to Jesus.

I believe there are dozens of reasons why it doesn't make sense to join Satan's team. But the one thing I want to do before we move on is simply to remind you that unless he has God's permission, Satan cannot touch those who belong to Christ.

That doesn't mean he won't try to make us think he's going to harm us or try to scare us in other ways. But there won't be any substance to it. Without God's permission, the worst he can do is some simple parlor tricks. And even if he pulls that, all we need to remember is our authority over him in the name of Jesus.

The Bible tells us that as Christians we have nothing to fear from the devil, because "the one who is in you is greater than the one who is in the world" (1 John 4:4).

And the book of Hebrews tells us that Jesus died so that "he might destroy him who holds the power of death—that is, the devil—and free those who all their lives were held in slavery by their fear of death" (2:14–15).

If we belong to Christ, the bottom line for us all is that we have absolutely nothing to fear from Satan. He can bluster and threaten all he wants, but we are always secure in God's protective hands.

5

Strange Lights in the Night Sky

DENVER, COLORADO. Just past ten P.M. Peggy Otis was driving down a quiet residential street with her young granddaughter, Jennifer, asleep beside her.

Suddenly something in the sky attracted her attention. It was an airplane, apparently coming in for a landing at Denver's Stapleton Airport. No. Wait a minute. It wasn't an airplane at all. It was much too low. It was going to crash into the street right in front of her!

Peggy remembers that "sparks were being emitted from underneath it, and it suddenly came down so low that I thought it was going to smash the top of my car. I screamed at Jennifer to wake up, and jumped out of the car. The craft was dome-shaped, and I could see someone moving inside it. We were terrified, thinking that it was going to crash us."

It didn't crash into Peggy's car, nor did it fall into the

street. Instead, after lingering for a few scary moments, it simply floated away. But before it did, something even stranger happened.

Someone from the craft spoke to her. She didn't hear an audible voice, but the message was strong and clear: "Don't forget us."

That was all. What could it have meant?

Later that evening, when Peggy told her husband what had happened, he called the airport to see if anyone else had reported seeing anything out of the ordinary. No one had. Mrs. Otis described the craft as making a noise like that of a garbage disposal and said that it came low enough that she could see people inside of it—and yet nobody else saw a thing.[1]

What was it that Peggy Otis saw that night in Denver? Whose voice did she hear?

COCHRAN COUNTY, TEXAS. The sheriff's department responded to an agitated call from a rancher who complained that "something" was killing his livestock. The rancher said the situation was so weird that he couldn't explain it over the phone.

When the sheriff went to investigate, the rancher drove him to a spot a couple of miles from the house, where a circle about thirty feet in diameter had been pressed into a wheat field. And there, in the middle of the circle, was a dead cow that had been butchered with surgical precision. Its tongue had been removed, along with its navel. Apart from the tongue, no other edible meat had been taken. Whoever had killed this animal was not interested in food, and they had not butchered it here. There was no blood on the ground.

About a quarter of a mile away from the cow, the men found a dead steer lying in the middle of another large circle. It had been butchered in exactly the same way, but there was something different here. Within the circle itself, the wheat had been burned down to within four inches of the ground. The only explanation was that something very hot had come out of the sky and almost landed here. Almost, but not quite—otherwise the wheat would have been burned completely to the ground.

The sheriff's subsequent investigation turned up nothing further, except for the fact that several area residents reported seeing "strange lights" in the sky around the time the animals had been killed.[2]

What happened in Denver, Colorado and in Cochran County, Texas?

IT'S AN OLD STORY, BUT IT'S GETTING MORE AND MORE WEIRD

A businessman named Kenneth Arnold first coined the term "flying saucers" way back in 1947. Arnold was describing some weird-looking aircraft he had seen from the cockpit of his private airplane.

Over the next several years, thousands of people all over the world reported seeing other strange aircraft maneuvering through our skies. Some were saucer-shaped, just like the ones Arnold saw, some were cigar-shaped, and still others seemed to be almost jelly-like, amorphous blobs that had no clearly defined shape. All agreed they were like no other aircraft they had ever seen. They flew at speeds estimated at several thousand miles per hour. Sometimes they hung almost dead still in the sky. Other times they shot up into the sky so fast that they completely disappeared from view within seconds. They also made impossible ninety-degree turns and could stop in an instant.

In 1948 some claimed a flying saucer had crashed in New Mexico, and that the air force had recovered bodies from the wreckage. The air force later issued an official statement saying that the crashed vehicle was not a spacecraft at all, but a harmless weather balloon. But many people didn't believe it. Some still don't.

By the mid-1950s several books had been written accusing the air force of trying to keep the American people from knowing what was really going on in the skies above us. Most of these authors felt that something other-worldly and sinister was behind the activity, and the air force was keeping a lid on it because the truth was too frightening for us to handle.

These authors also believed that "something big" was just around the corner. They felt that the secrecy was going to end, and we'd all know the truth about these unidentified flying objects—probably by 1959 or 1960 at the latest. More than likely, they said, the government was going to announce that we had made contact with advanced beings from a nearby planet, probably Venus or Mars.

It didn't happen. Here we are forty years later and we don't really know any more about flying saucers than we did when Kenneth Arnold reportedly saw the first. We don't know where they come from. We don't know what they're made of. We don't know why or even if they're really here.

But one thing we do know is that the reports won't go away. Thousands of sightings are reported to authorities every year. UFO investigator Alan Hynek says that since Arnold's day there have been a minimum of seven hundred thousand sightings in the United States alone, and millions worldwide.[3]

Over the years, the sightings have changed. Now strange circles are supposedly being burned into grain fields here and in Europe. There are numerous reports of cattle mutilations. And even more interesting, sightings have become much more personal. Millions of people throughout the world claim that they have made contact with aliens from deep space—many of them against their will. UFO researcher Clifford Wilson says he believes there are 50,000 cases of these "Close Encounters of the Third Kind" on record.[4]

WHO ARE THEY AND WHAT DO THEY WANT WITH US?

Some alien abductees report having medical experiments performed upon them. They say the aliens seem especially interested in the human reproductive system. Others tell of being chased and taken aboard spacecraft against their will. Some say they'll never again sleep without a light on.

Of course, all of this is disturbing. But what is even more disturbing is that a growing number of people have been "given messages" to deliver on behalf of the aliens. Most of the messages have to do with love, peace, and learning to live in harmony with each other. On the surface, that all sounds very good.

But underneath there's a secondary message that sounds strangely familiar: "You are gods. Learn to unlock the power within you. Throw off the shackles of your narrow-minded religions (especially Christianity) and join us in experiencing your divine godhead." The message is identical to what permeates so much of the occult—such as those delivered by the false angels we talked about in chapter 2.

What is even more coincidental is that thousands of people throughout the world now claim to be making contact with beings from space through meditation, channeling, automatic writing, and similar methods that are occultic in nature. It seems odd that any "advanced civilization" would resort to these questionable and unreliable means of delivering an important message to us. But then again, the messages we're receiving from these "aliens" aren't exactly trustworthy.

Going back to the early days of close encounters, we almost always find that the UFOnauts claimed to be from Venus, Mars, or one of the other nearby planets. But since science now indicates there are no advanced civilizations on nearby worlds, the aliens have simply changed their story. Now they come from Zeta Reticuli, Wolf 24, Alpha Centauri, or some other far distant region of the universe. Areas that, coincidentally enough, we cannot check out.

Even if aliens did come from somewhere in the neighborhood of Alpha Centauri, which is the nearest star, it would take them 80,000 years to get here by conventional means. Even traveling at the speed of light, it would take hundreds or even thousands of years to get here from most points in space. To get here any sooner means they would have to travel faster than the speed of light, which the laws of physics tell us is absolutely impossible.

AND SINCE WE'RE TALKING SCIENCE . . .

Astrophysicist Hugh Ross, founder and president of the organization Reason to Believe, has spent years analyzing hundreds of UFO sightings. Dr. Ross says that people are definitely seeing something unusual. Even though 95 percent of all sightings are eventually explained as cases of mistaken identity, there are still far too many unexplained sightings to write the whole thing off as weather balloons, swamp gas, and the like.

But having said that, Hugh Ross also believes that the 5 percent of legitimate UFOs cannot possibly be physical objects. If they were, they would have to follow the laws of physics—and they don't.

Here are ten reasons from Hugh Ross as to why UFOs are not physical objects:[5]

1. No physical artifacts have been recovered.

Despite numerous rumors of crashes, captures, and other close encounters with unidentified flying objects, Dr. Ross says that to date there is not one documented case of physical evidence being collected. If UFOs were physical objects, fifty-plus years of visiting Planet Earth most certainly would have resulted in some sort of physical evidence being left behind.

2. Some UFOs have been seen but could not be photographed. Others have been photographed even though nothing could be seen.

Dr. Ross says the same thing has happened with radar. On occasion, UFOs have been plainly seen hovering in the sky, but radar screens at nearby airports or military installations don't show a thing. At other times, radar has picked up strong signals from craft moving through the sky, but nothing has been spotted visually. It is impossible for physical objects to behave in this way.

3. UFOs do not create sonic booms.

If you've ever lived anywhere near an air force base, you know the thunderous boom that occurs when a supersonic jet breaks the sound barrier. It shakes the house. Occasionally it breaks windows. And yet UFOs travel in and out of our atmosphere at speeds many times faster than sound, and they do it in complete silence. According to the laws of physics, that's impossible.

4. UFOs have been seen making ninety-degree turns at speeds estimated in excess of 18,000 miles per hour.

Solid aircraft simply could not survive such turns, nor could any creatures inside of them. A person who was inside a spacecraft that did make a turn like that would have to be scraped off the walls with a spatula. A solid ball of steel cannot survive a right-angle turn at only 5,000 miles per hour. Nothing can survive such a turn at 18,000 miles per hour.

5. UFOs have been observed to change shape, size, and color at random.

A solid object cannot change instantaneously from an oval to a circle to a square and back to an oval. Liquid, yes. Gas, yes. But a solid, no. And yet UFOs have been observed to do all of these things and more.

6. UFOs have been performing a number of other maneuvers that are physically impossible.

For example, on one occasion two UFOs were reportedly seen traveling at a high rate of speed directly toward each other. Observers on the ground braced themselves for a disastrous crash, but it never came. Instead, the two objects simply merged into one larger craft. After a few minutes, they separated again. During another sighting, a large UFO suddenly split into five smaller objects, which then came back together. UFOs have also disappeared and then reappeared, and they have disintegrated only to "reintegrate" a few moments later as if nothing had happened. How is it that objects traveling thousands of miles per hour merge without causing so much as a dent in each other? It can't happen. Not to physical objects. And yet according to what dozens of witnesses have reported, it does.

7. No communication between UFOs has ever been detected.

If "flying saucers" were interplanetary spacecraft, we almost certainly would have intercepted communications between them. But even though we have had our ears tuned to the skies for decades, we haven't heard a thing. Instead, these craft speed through our skies in complete silence. This brings up another interesting point. If these objects really came from deep space, their arrival would have been recorded by some of the world's many top observatories. And yet, even though there are dozens of extremely high-powered telescopes in observatories around the world, none of them has ever recorded an image of a craft approaching the earth from space. Nobody sees them coming. All of a sudden they're just here.

8. Some UFOs have been seen shooting out "finite" beams of light.

In other words, a beam of light that goes out so far and just stops. But light simply does not behave that way. It keeps going, either until it is stopped by a solid object, such as a wall, or, if there is no object to stop it, until its energy is dissipated. According to Dr. Ross, this is just another of the many things UFOs do that are not compatible with the rules that govern our physical universe.

9. Although thousands of photographs of UFOs have

been taken over the years, none are of high quality.

Have you ever seen a clear photo of a UFO that was not later revealed to be a hoax? I haven't. They're always blurry. My first inclination would be to believe that the blurring was intentional on the part of the photographer, who was trying to perpetrate a fraud. But then, some of these photographs are of objects that have been seen by dozens or even hundreds of people, so that rules out deception. And yet if the UFOs were real, physical, solid objects, they wouldn't blur this way—especially the ones that were stationary or slow-moving. Think about how many photos you have seen of the space shuttle lifting off from Cape Canaveral. Were they blurry? More than likely, they were crisp, clear, and sharp, even though the shuttle was traveling at a high rate of speed. Ross says that physical objects simply do not blur the way UFOs do when they are photographed. The fault doesn't lie with the photographs or the photographers, but with the objects themselves. They appear blurry on film because they *are* blurry. They aren't real in the sense that they aren't solid physical objects.

10. Magnetic field measurements do not concur with magnetic disturbances that are taking place.

UFOs have reportedly caused disruption of earthbound communications. They have made car engines stall, induced power blackouts, caused clocks and watches to stop dead in their tracks, and so on. And yet when we have tried to measure the electromagnetic energy that has caused this to happen, it's simply not there. In other words, Dr. Ross says, something "real" is taking place, but it's not physical. If it were, we could measure it.

WHERE DO UFOs *REALLY* COME FROM?

But if UFOs aren't physical, what are they? Why are they here? And where have they come from?

Space aliens, whoever they really are, seem to be intensely religious people, and they are zealous in spreading their view of the universe. Over and over again they urge us earthlings to open our hearts to the universe through meditation and other mystical practices. They seem quite comfortable with Eastern-style religious practices and quite in agreement with many of the components of the New Age movement.

In fact, the only religion they seem to disdain is Christianity, which they label as narrow-minded and divisive. They have no problem throwing Christ's name around, but they have zero tolerance when he is mentioned as the only begotten Son of God who died to save us from our sins.

All indications are that UFOs represent a supernatural phenomenon of a far different kind. It's highly unlikely that the UFOs zipping through our skies are interplanetary spacecraft.

UFO investigator John Keel says:

> Thousands of mediums, psychics, and UFO contactees have been receiving mountains of messages from 'Ashtar' in recent years. Mr. Ashtar represents himself as

a leader in the great intergalactic councils that hold regular meetings on Jupiter, Venus, Saturn, and many planets known to us. But Ashtar is not a new arrival. Variations of this name, such as Astaroth, Ashar, Asharoth, etc., appear in demonological literature throughout history, both in the Orient and the Occident. Mr. Ashtar has been around a very long time, posting as assorted gods and demons and now, in the modern phase, as another glorious spaceman.[6]

Who is Ashtar? One of the pagan gods the Israelites were commanded not to worship when they entered the Promised Land. God told His people that when they came into Canaan they were to "break down their altars, smash their sacred stones and burn their Asherah poles in the fire" (Deut. 12:3). Asherah is another name for Ashtar.

That alone ought to make us skittish of who is really behind the whole UFO phenomenon.

Jacques Vallee is one of the world's most noted UFO investigators. He holds a master's degree in astrophysics and a Ph.D. in computer science. He has addressed the United Nations on the topic of UFOs and was the inspiration for the character LaCombe in the film *Close Encounters of the Third Kind.*

During the years Dr. Vallee has been involved in UFO research, he has carefully analyzed hundreds of the most baffling sightings and written several books on the subject.

When he first began investigating UFOs, he wasn't convinced there was anything mysterious or sinister about them. Most of the sightings, he figured, would be fairly easy to explain as a simple misinterpretation of data. If UFOs were real physical objects, the most plausible explanation would be that they came from other planets.

Today, Dr. Vallee is convinced that UFOs are real. But he's no longer certain they come from other planets.

He writes that during his years of researching the subject of UFOs, "I had become aware of some pretty shady business behind the apparently harmless antics of the contactee groups. Now I wanted to focus my attention on the problem at hand: the question of who was doing all this and what their designs on us might be."[7]

I don't know anything about Dr. Vallee's spiritual beliefs. If he believes in God, he is not outspoken about it. In everything he does, he tries to be the consummate scientist—completely open-minded, judging every bit of evidence on its own merits. And yet in his book *Messengers of Deception* he has proposed the idea that UFOs are part of a master plan to sweep away the earth's old social order, including all existing religions, to make room for the new. He writes:

> Let me summarize my conclusions thus far. UFOs are real. They are an application of psychotronic technology; that is, they are physical devices used to affect human consciousness. They may not be from outer space; they may, in fact, be terrestrial-based manipulating devices. Their purpose may be to achieve social

changes on this planet. Their methods are those of deception: systematic manipulation of witnesses and contactees; covert use of various sects and cult control of the channels through which the alleged "space messages" can make an impact on the public.[8]

Dr. Vallee also says, "I think we have a very real UFO problem."[9]

Over the years, he has interviewed dozens of people who claim to have made contact with or received messages from beings whom they believed came from other worlds. Almost universally, these people talked about the importance of establishing a unified one-world government that would put an end to wars and rumors of wars. They are excited about the potential of a new economic system in which money will be eliminated and all people everywhere will share equally in the planet's worth. And they talk about a new worldwide religion that would reveal the true nature of the universe and free us from all our old, outmoded notions of eternal truth. In many ways it sounds exactly like the social and political climate of the one-world government spoken of in Revelation.

Dr. Jacques Vallee is not the only one who believes the aliens—or whoever they are—are trying to bring about a change in our society. Dr. Alan Hynek, whose credentials include his tenure as chairman of the astronomy department of Northwestern University, writes:

I have the impression that the UFOs are announcing a change that is coming soon in our scientific paradigms. I am very much afraid that the UFOs are related to psychic phenomena.

Certainly the phenomenon has psychic aspects. I don't talk about them very much because to a general audience the words "psychic" and "occult" have bad overtones. They say, "Aw, it's all crazy." But the fact is that there are psychic things; for instance, UFOs seem to materialize and dematerialize. There are people who've had UFO experiences who've claimed to have developed psychic ability. There have been reported healings in close encounters and there have been reported cases of precognition, where people had foreknowledge or forewarning that they were going to see something. There has been a change of outlook, a change of philosophy of persons' lives. Now, you see, those are rather tricky things to talk about openly, but it's there.[10]

Ronald Story, in his book *Guardians of the Universe?* adds, "It can be said, with certainty, that a 'conditioning process' is taking place, which is either directly or indirectly related to the UFO phenomenon."[11]

OCCULTLIKE EXPERIENCES

It seems obvious that many people are ready and willing to believe any message that comes from space. After all, the reasoning goes, if these beings are so technologically advanced that they can travel billions of miles through space, it only makes sense that they are also far advanced in philosophy, religion, and personal morality.

That's the type of thinking that sent Whitley Strieber's book *Communion* rocketing to the top of the bestseller lists for several weeks in 1987. It told of Strieber's encounters with strange beings who often invaded his home in the middle of the night. Prior to these uninvited visits, he sometimes saw lights in the sky, so Strieber naturally assumed that his strange visitors came from outer space. Wherever they came from, their visits always left him feeling depressed, angry, and worried about the safety of his wife and young son.

Initially Strieber didn't remember anything about these intruders. He only knew that he was experiencing panic attacks and felt troubled by bits and pieces of strange memories that made no sense—such as looking up into huge almond-shaped eyes as he lay frightened in his bed. It was only through hypnosis that he remembered the full scope of what had been happening to him.

To Strieber's amazement, he received hundreds of letters from readers saying they had undergone similar experiences. They told him he was reporting their own stories in exacting detail, right down to the almond-shaped eyes of the intruders.

Certainly Whitley Strieber's stories about strange beings from outer space invading his home in the middle of the night are scary. But there is something even more troublesome. In *Transformation*, his follow-up to *Communion*, Strieber writes, "Maybe the visitors are gods. Maybe they created us."[12]

He goes on to say that one of the creatures "seemed almost angelic to me, so pure and so full of knowledge."[13]

When Strieber asked the creatures why they were here, they responded that they had come to "recycle souls."[14]

Over time, as Whitley Strieber's relationship with his strange "friends" deepened, so did his foray into the world of the occult. He had out-of-body experiences and was able during one of them to visit with his long-dead father. He became involved in shamanism, which he describes as "the oldest of all human religious traditions," and Wicca, which is otherwise known as witchcraft, although he protested that it has "no connection to satanism or other perversions."

It is not surprising that Strieber's encounter with "aliens" led him into the world of the occult. Dr. Hugh Ross has interviewed many people who claim to have been abducted by aliens, and he says he found that every one of them had been involved in the occult prior to their abduction. There is simply no way the connection between the occult and UFO encounters can be reasonably denied.

Strieber has come to believe that the appearance of his "visitors" has a strong connection to ancient—non-Christian—religions, and writes that "we have a life in another form—and it is on that level of reality that the visitors are primarily present."[15]

To any student of the occult, the most frightening of Strieber's comments is this:

What is interesting to me now is how to develop effective techniques to call them [the visitors] into one's life and make use of what they have to offer. . . . The most effective technique seems to be simply to open oneself, asking for what one needs the most without placing any conditions at all on what they might be.[16]

But if I open myself up to one of these beings, who am I really inviting into my life?

Are these creatures who come in UFOs humankind's saviors, as they claim to be? Do they really want to lead us to an era of peace and enlightenment?

Or are they simply an old deception wearing new clothes? Not natural but *super*natural, not extraterrestrial but extra*dimensional*—finding a new way to deceive, control, and torment?

Unfortunately, when the facts are closely examined, they speak for themselves.

6

Voices From Beyond the Grave

Rhonda, her parents, and her older brother lived in a pleasant, middle-class neighborhood. Rhonda got good grades in school. She was a member of the pep squad. She and her friends liked to spend a lot of time at the mall, checking out the latest fashions and—as would be expected of most fifteen-year-old girls—the boys.

All of that was changed by the news that her mom was seriously ill. At first Rhonda refused to believe it, even though her mother was growing visibly weaker and sicker on an almost daily basis. As it turned out, the illness was devastating and swift. Three months after she was diagnosed, Rhonda's mother died at the age of thirty-eight.

Rhonda wasn't comforted by her pastor's assurances that her mother was in heaven and that they would be able to see each other again "someday." Rhonda needed her mother "right now." How she longed to hear her voice. Even hearing Mom telling her to clean up her room would have been paradise.

Rhonda cried a lot. She didn't do her homework. She was no longer interested in hanging out with the other kids from her neighborhood.

And that was when one of her friends introduced her to the Ouija Board. Rhonda was skeptical at first when her friend suggested that she could use the board to contact her mother "in heaven." Rhonda didn't know much about the Ouija Board. She'd always considered it to be nothing more than a child's toy. But because she desperately wanted to talk to her mother, she finally decided to give it a try.

As her best friend sat across from her, Rhonda rested her fingers on the plastic pointer and asked her mother's spirit to speak to her. The answer was dramatic and immediate. The pointer began to fly all over the board, spelling out messages from Rhonda's mom.

I've missed you so much!

Please don't cry for me, because I'm very happy here.

And so on.

Tears of joy rolled down Rhonda's cheeks as she and her mother chatted happily together about things that were important to the two of them. It was such a comfort to know that she hadn't lost her mother after all.

The next day Rhonda couldn't wait to get home from school to talk with her mother again. The day after that she didn't even go to school.

As time went by, the pattern intensified. Rhonda spent more and more time with her mother and less and less time with anyone else. At first her dad, deep in his own grief, didn't realize that his daughter was withdrawing from life. But after a while he noticed that the phone had stopped ringing, as Rhonda's friends began to leave her alone. She had turned down their invitations so many times that they simply stopped trying. He did receive calls from his daughter's teachers, who were concerned that Rhonda's grades were slipping drastically. She was missing quite a bit of school, and when she did come she seemed to spend most of her time by herself.

Meanwhile, still speaking through the Ouija Board, Rhonda's "mother" didn't seem the least bit concerned that her daughter's life was falling apart. She never asked how her grades were coming along. Never expressed a desire that her daughter should go out with her friends and enjoy herself. Didn't for a moment suggest that a girl her age ought to spend more time with the living than with the dead.

Instead, "she" was content to lead her daughter deeper and deeper into the world of the supernatural. She introduced Rhonda to a number of her "friends" from the spirit world. Talked with her about developing her "psychic powers" and brought "spirit guides" into her life.

I'd like to tell you that Rhonda's story has a happy ending—but I can't. The last time I saw her, she was gaunt, hollow-eyed, seemingly lost to this world. That was probably fifteen years ago. Since then, I have lost touch with her.

I think about her sometimes, and with those thoughts comes a deep sadness and anger. I pray for her and hope she has found her way back to "reality," but I have no way of knowing for sure.

I don't believe that Rhonda was ever in contact with her mother's departed spirit. She was talking to someone who knew her very well, someone who also knew her mother very well, but whoever it was, it was *not* her mother. Now let's see if I can back up that statement.

A CLOSER LOOK AT THE OUIJA BOARD

What does the Ouija Board look like? It is a flat, smooth board with letters and numbers on it, along with the words "Yes," "No," "Hello," and "Good-bye." The "players," usually two people who sit across the board from each other, place their hands lightly on a planchette, or pointer, which moves around the board, landing momentarily on letters and numbers to spell out answers to whatever questions are asked.

These boards have been around for a long, long time—some scholars say since at least 600 years before Christ was born. Today, the board is marketed as a toy. You can find Ouija Boards on the shelves of stores like Toys R Us, alongside board games such as Monopoly and Scrabble. In fact, in a poll of readers conducted by *Zillions* magazine, the Ouija Board tied with Monopoly as the favorite board game of children.

Yet, as Rhonda's experience shows, the Ouija Board is not a toy.

Some experts dismiss the Ouija Board as a fraud. Other psychologists who have studied it believe the pointer is moved across the board through the power of the subconscious mind. In other words, the person who is using the board is asking questions with his conscious mind and answering them with his subconscious. In extreme cases, they believe, this can result in a psychotic break and even in schizophrenia.

Although this may occasionally be the case, my research and personal experience don't hesitate to place this "toy" in an even more dangerous category. I tend to agree with occult expert Edmond Gruss, who says, "The content of the message often goes beyond that which can be reasonably explained as something from the conscious or subconscious mind of the operator." He goes on to say,

> The board has been subjected to tests which support supernatural intervention. The testing of the board was presented in an article by Sir William Barrett, in the September 1914 *Proceedings of the American Society for Psychical Research* (pp. 381–394). The Barrett report indicated that the board worked efficiently with the operators blindfolded, the board's alphabet rearranged, and its surface hidden from the sight of those working it. It worked with such speed and accuracy under these tests that Barrett concluded: "Reviewing the results as a whole, I am convinced of their supernormal character,

and that we have here an exhibition of some intelligent, disincarnate agency mingling with the personality of one or more of the sitters and guiding their muscular movements."[1]

Many who have studied the Ouija Board believe it is a means of communicating with voices from beyond. Here's what God has to say about that:

> Let no one be found among you who . . . practices divination or sorcery, interprets omens, engages in witchcraft, or casts spells, or who is a medium or spiritist or who consults the dead. Anyone who does these things is detestable to the Lord. (Deut. 18:10–12)

Pretty strong words. But why? Why is God so angry at this practice?

DESIRE TO DECEIVE

We've already seen that there are beings "out there" anxious and ready to communicate with us any time we are willing to open our minds to them. Sometimes they present themselves as angels. Other times as beings from other planets. And on still other occasions as the disembodied spirits of loved ones who have died. But I believe these voices "whispering in the wind" come from none of these places.

It is more likely that they are the voices of demons who are anxious to lead us away from biblical truth and whose ultimate aim is to bring us into supernatural bondage. They seem to know just about everything there is to know about us, and they cleverly use that information to convince us of their authenticity and win our confidence.

The fact that they know so much about us doesn't surprise me. I think demons make it a point to learn as much about us as they possibly can. They are always watching us, looking for vulnerabilities and weaknesses so they can attack to bring us down. After all, they're trying to win a war.

And because of this, people who play with the Ouija Board sometimes pay a steep price for their involvement. Gruss writes,

> The many cases of "possession" after a period of Ouija Board use also support the claim that supernatural contact is made through the board. Psychics and parapsychologists have received letters from hundreds of people who have experienced "possession" (an invasion of their personalities). Rev. Donald Page, a well-known clairvoyant and exorcist of the Christian Spiritualist Church, is reported as saying that most of his "possession" cases "are people who have used the Ouija Board," and that "this is one of the easiest and quickest ways to become possessed."[2]

My own experience with the Ouija Board was short. In fact, it lasted less than an hour, but I think it says something crucial about the power behind the device.

I was in junior high school when a friend brought his

Ouija Board to school. We spent some time playing with it during lunch, and it was working like gangbusters—the pointer was flying all over the place answering our questions. I thought it was pretty cool, so I asked my friend if I could borrow the board. He said yes.

That evening I asked my dad if he'd like to check it out with me. He didn't know much about Ouija Boards either, but said that he'd give it a shot. We sat down at the dining room table to try it out, but we couldn't get it to respond. Rather than answer our questions, as it had done so quickly at school, the pointer simply sat there. It didn't move at all. Needless to say, I was more than a little disappointed.

It wasn't until the next day that my mother told me she had been afraid of that board the moment I brought it through the door. She didn't want it in her house, and so the entire time my dad and I had been playing with it, she had been in the next room praying for our protection. I'm convinced that's why the board wouldn't work. God's power was there in a special way, and whatever forces were responsible for the board's operation couldn't get anywhere near us!

I'm not alone in thinking that Ouija Boards are dangerous. In his book *Channeling,* author Jon Klimo, who mostly takes an unbiblical view of communication with spirits and other entities and insists on the positive value of such experiences, writes,

> The device has a reputation for attracting the lowest class of channeled entities. It is reported that one can

contact a hodgepodge of hucksters and tricksters "coming through." In the most comprehensive study to date, *Ouija: The Most Dangerous Game*, Stoker Hunt writes, "Because of the intimate nature of the information revealed, the Ouija Board is incredibly seductive. . . ." Hunt presents a sobering gallery of cases in which individuals reportedly relinquished personal judgment, lost control, even killed loved ones, under the direction of invisible guides of the Ouija Board. "In early stages of obsession or possession, the victim becomes increasingly reliant on the Ouija Board. He craves more and more revelations."

Psychic authority Susy Smith agrees: "Warn people away from the Ouija Board . . . until you have learned to be fully protected."[3]

THE RISE OF SPIRITUALISM

Attempting to communicate with the dead is nothing new. It's been going on for thousands of years, as shown by the passage from Deuteronomy quoted earlier in this chapter. But the modern American "Spiritualist" movement sprang from the alleged experiences of two sisters in 1848.

Margaret and Kate Fox were fourteen and twelve when their family moved into a small house in the town of Hydesville, New York. The family later reported that they got little sleep during the first three months in their new home. They were kept awake at night by various rapping and banging noises that seemed to come from somewhere inside the walls.

Eventually, the family decided to try to communicate with whoever—or whatever—was making the noises. Mrs. Fox asked the entity if it knew the ages of her seven children. It quickly responded by correctly rapping out the ages of all of them, including a three-year-old who had died.

Mrs. Fox then asked, "Is this a human being that answers my questions correctly?"

There was no response.

"Is it a spirit? If it is, make two raps."

She wrote, "Two sounds were given as soon as the request was made."

Eventually the "spirit" identified itself as a peddler named Charles B. Rosna, who said he had been murdered in the house.

Before long the fame of the Fox family—and especially Margaret and Kate, who seemed to be the center of this spiritual activity—had spread throughout the region. The girls eventually began to give public performances in which messages "from the dead" were given to the audience through means of the rapping, banging noises.

In their book *The Afterlife*, psychic investigators Jenny Randles and Peter Hough write,

> The press loved this new sensation. In 1849 the girls gave their first public performance in Rochester, then toured other towns in the eastern states. It was like a contagion. Other mediums joined the throng—the mainstay of this fledgling religion. Before long "spirit

rapping" had spread across the entire United States, then over to Europe and Britain. This was the generation of Spiritualism—a movement built around the psychic abilities of two teenage girls.[4]

(Interestingly enough, rapping continues to be a significant feature of "supernatural communication." Whitley Strieber writes of attending a ceremony where he and his friends heard loud rapping noises, which they assumed were being produced by unseen entities.)

In 1851 three professors from Buffalo University investigated the Fox sisters, including their younger sister, Leah, who had become a significant part of the story. They concluded that fraudulent methods had been used to generate the rapping sounds. However, these conclusions did not diminish the sisters' popularity. In fact, among their many fans was Sir Arthur Conan Doyle, creator of Sherlock Holmes, who became a convinced Spiritualist and spent the last dozen years of his life deeply involved in the occult.

As for the sisters themselves, their involvement in Spiritualism did not have a happy ending. Jon Klimo writes,

All three Fox sisters married, some more than once; all, to varying degrees, sought refuge in alcohol. Margaret became an alcoholic. Thirty years after it had all begun, their relationships with each other had badly deteriorated. Leah had turned Catholic and was trying to take custody of Kate's two children. Margaret, who had sided with Kate, published a letter in the New York

Tribune, in which she severed her ties with Spiritualism and claimed the whole thing had been a fraud. To get back at Leah, Kate joined Margaret in this confession. A year later, Margaret completely reversed herself, saying that the initial fraud exposé was done for money, under the influence of anti-Spiritualists. But the damage had been done, and it was ample ammunition for the press and disbelievers. Shortly thereafter, within three years of one another, all three sisters died.[5]

Despite the sad ending to the Fox sisters' story, Randles and Hough write that during the second half of the nineteenth century, Spiritualism experienced tremendous growth:

> Spiritualism embraced other phenomena beyond spirit rapping. Telekinesis—the paranormal movement of objects, including furniture—was the most common. Occasionally, hands formed out of a substance called ectoplasm were seen manipulating objects. Indeed, entire entities were observed to be formed from such material, entities that were able to converse with those present.
>
> There were also "direct voice" mediums. Here, the disembodied voice of the deceased could be heard in the seance room. Musical instruments would play themselves and levitate around the sitters. "Spirit guides" became the vogue, too. Usually the deceased spirits of children or Indians, they took control of the medium. Whilst the medium was in a trance, the guide would take over the body and make use of the vocal cords.

Many of the systems of communication with the after-life developed then are still used by mediums today, although they tend to be less theatrical.[6]

Do I believe that these were all legitimate supernatural experiences? For the most part, no. I believe most mediums are hucksters, making a buck by exploiting another's grief. It's interesting to note that the world-renowned magician Harry Houdini spent a great deal of time proving the fakery of many of the spiritists of his day. In fact, he promised his wife that when he died, if there was any possible way to communicate with her, he would do it. The two of them arranged a special code which was known only to them. Interestingly enough, after Houdini died, his widow never received a single message that led her to believe her husband was attempting to communicate with her.

But even though I believe most spiritists are fakes, the warning in Deuteronomy still stands. This is a dangerous area, one that demonic forces are all too happy to exploit.

Randles and Hough try hard to be objective in their investigation of the afterlife, but show their bias against traditional Christian beliefs when they write about the reasons Spiritualism grew: "The dawning technological age caused many people to turn away from Christianity toward a religion more suited to the times. Christianity seemed antiquated in an age where things needed to be tested and evaluated on evidence—not just accepted as some 'whimsical' belief."[7]

There it is again. "Christianity is old and outdated. It's

time to make way for the new." And yet Jesus himself said, "Heaven and earth will pass away, but my words will never pass away" (Matt. 24:35).

It seems to me that we are faced with a choice. Do we accept the words of entities who claim to be the spirits of dead loved ones—or do we accept the words of Jesus Christ?

Ben Alexander feels the same way. Alexander was once a prominent British medium, but now heads up a Christian organization called Exposing Satan's Power. Alexander was a member of the Christian Spiritualist Church, which attempted to merge Christianity and occult practices. This church featured in its services many of the practices you'd expect to find in any Bible-believing congregation—hymn-singing, preaching, reading of the Scriptures, even Communion. But every gathering also featured a seance led by Alexander or another accomplished medium.

The church taught that Jesus Christ was the greatest spirit medium who ever lived and pointed to the Bible's account of His transfiguration as proof. During this event, Moses and Elijah suddenly appeared with Jesus and He talked to them (see Matt. 17:1–5). What Alexander and the others in his church failed to understand was that this was a one-time experience in which God was illustrating that Jesus' authority is greater than Moses or any of the other prophets who came before Him.

As Alexander continued reading the Bible, he began to be troubled by Scriptures that could not be reconciled with the beliefs and practices of his church. He was especially bothered by passages like these:

Do not turn to mediums or seek out spiritists, for you will be defiled by them. I am the Lord your God. (Lev. 19:31)

A man or woman who is a medium or spiritist among you must be put to death. You are to stone them; their blood will be on their own heads. (Lev. 20:27)

When men tell you to consult mediums and spiritists, who whisper and mutter, should not a people inquire of their God? Why consult the dead on behalf of the living? (Isa. 8:19)

As God began to awaken his heart, Ben Alexander became convinced that he had never really been in contact with the spirits of departed loved ones. The beings who spoke through him were clever mimics. Their performances were almost flawlessly convincing, but Alexander was certain that was all they were—performances.

He says that he could sense the displeasure of his spirit guides whenever he tried to spend time reading the Bible. He remembers that on one occasion an unseen force ripped the Bible out of his hands and threw it across the room. Another time the pages started to spin rapidly and then began to be ripped out and tossed into the air. Instead of trying to explain away the Bible's prohibitions against communicating with the dead, Alexander's spirits were openly showing anger and contempt toward the Word of God.

Eventually Alexander decided to surrender himself to Christ. He also decided that he needed to make a public profession of his new faith and follow the Lord's command to be baptized. The spirits were really angry now. In fact, on one occasion, he found a threatening message written, apparently by finger, on his car's fogged windshield: "We'll be waiting for you on the other side," it said. "We'll get you then."

But for all their bluster, the spirits never bothered Alexander again. He is convinced that his Lord is protecting him, and he is not worried at all about what awaits him "on the other side." He knows that when he dies, he will go to be with Jesus. Today, he also knows why the Bible warns against attempting to communicate with the dead. It is opening oneself up to the possibility of invasion by sinister forces.

Following his conversion to Christianity, Alexander moved to the United States, where he has built a successful ministry. Well into his seventies, he still spends most of his time on the road, lecturing about the dangers of involvement in the occult. Occasionally he travels back to London, where he tries to share the gospel with some of his remaining medium friends. Unfortunately, he finds that most of them are still bewildered by his "defection," and they see no reason to change their behavior.

Ben Alexander's story adds an exclamation point to the fact that there is no way to reconcile what the Bible teaches with the practice of communicating with the dead.

THE WEIRD SAGA OF A GHOST NAMED PHILIP

It all started in 1972 when several members of the Toronto Society for Psychical Research wanted to see if they could create their own ghost and get it to manifest itself to them. They decided that the ghost's name would be Philip, and that he had lived and died in seventeenth-century England. They even hired a writer to put together a fictional biography and asked him to make his account as heroic and romantic as possible. An artist also was commissioned to produce Philip's portrait. Following this, the members of the group were asked to learn everything they could about this fictional character, after which they would attempt to contact him on "the other side."

They tried for several months to communicate with Philip, without receiving so much as a whisper in reply. No surprise there. Philip had never existed. But as it turned out, that didn't matter.

One night, as the members of the group sat around a table calling out, "Hello, Philip!" something decided to make its presence known. A number of sharp raps sounded from somewhere inside the table.

In subsequent gatherings, it didn't take much coaxing to get "Philip" to reappear. He quickly answered questions from the group by rapping on the table. He never contradicted what had been written about him, although members of the group reported that he occasionally added details of his own. Sometimes the group would sing to Philip, and when they did, he joined in by bouncing the table up and down.

Finally, Philip was introduced to the world through a television program, taped in front of a live audience at Toronto City Television studios. Traditional knowledge says that ghosts love the dark, but Philip wasn't the least bit bothered by television cameras and bright lights. When the show's moderator introduced him, he responded in the usual way—by rapping loudly on the table. And then the table began bouncing and bumping around on the stage, like something out of *Fantasia*.

For the next several minutes, Philip politely answered questions from several panelists and even members of the studio audience. He only fell silent when a member of the group that had "created" him challenged his existence.

"We only made you up, you know," the man said.

Upon hearing that lack of faith, Philip stopped talking, and no amount of coaxing could bring him back. It was only after members of the Toronto group redoubled their efforts to believe in him that Philip agreed to make a curtain call.[8]

This story brings up some intriguing questions: Who was Philip? Was he merely a product of the energy of the human mind? Or was his appearance the result of demonic activity? Had some demon, tricked into believing that Philip was a real person, decided to use Philip as a means of getting his own message across? Interesting questions. But whatever our conclusion, it does not negate God's severe warning in Deuteronomy: "Let no one be found among you who . . . is a medium or a spiritist or who consults the dead. Anyone who does these things is detestable to the Lord" (Deut. 18:10–12).

WHAT IS AUTOMATIC WRITING?

Another way spirits of the dead supposedly communicate with the living is through what is known as "automatic writing." This procedure involves holding a pen or pencil loosely in your hand and letting "the spirits" move it across the paper.

Some experts say that almost anyone who is willing to yield himself to the spirits can learn to be adept at automatic writing. All it takes is the ability to relax, empty yourself of conscious thought—sound familiar?—and allow the spirits to speak through you.

As you can imagine, the same dangers that are associated with Ouija Boards are also connected to automatic writing. Even those who believe that it is merely the power of the subconscious mind that takes control warn that a psychotic break and mental illness can result. Dr. J. B. Rhine, a Duke University psychologist who spent many years investigating occult phenomena, dismissed automatic writing as spontaneous "motor automatisms" and believed that it was caused by inner conflicts, repressions, and obsessions that came to the surface during the process.[9] This may be true in some cases, but automatic writing does involve opening oneself up to the possibility of invasion by supernatural forces.

And many of the messages received through automatic writing are in exact agreement with messages that are being passed on through spirit mediums, "angelic" visitors, and beings who supposedly come from outer space. Again and again, Christ is hailed as a great teacher but *never* as the Savior. Frequently, we are urged to unlock the power that lies within us. And we are told that the afterworld is a peaceful, happy place for everyone, regardless of what has been done or believed in this life. In other words, we're told that we might as well chuck the Bible out a window, because what it says doesn't really matter.

TEST THE SPIRITS

Today, more than ever before, many distinct voices vie for our attention. So it is vitally important to know how to tell a legitimate spiritual message from a counterfeit.

Author Phil Phillips gives five practical scriptural methods to "test the spirits."[10] He writes that an authentic messenger from God

(1) always proclaims—and never denies—that Jesus is God's Son and that He came to earth in fleshly form;

(2) always exalts Jesus Christ and points toward His atonement for sin, which He made when He died on the cross;

(3) never encourages divination or occult practices;

(4) never contradicts Scripture or dismisses its importance;

(5) never undermines the majesty, glory, or holiness of almighty God, King of the universe.

Good advice. And perfectly in line with what the apostle John wrote to us in 1 John 4:1–3:

Dear friends, do not believe every spirit, but test the spirits to see whether they are from God, because many false prophets have gone out into the world. This is how you can recognize the Spirit of God: Every spirit that acknowledges that Jesus Christ has come in the flesh is from God, but every spirit that does not acknowledge Jesus is not from God. This is the spirit of the antichrist, which you have heard is coming and even now is already in the world.

There are many reasons why people attempt to communicate with the dead. It's terribly difficult to lose a loved one, and, like Rhonda, whose story was told at the beginning of this chapter, the bereaved may long for reassurance that their loved ones are well and happy "on the other side." But as we've seen, attempting to communicate with the dead is forbidden by God because it opens a door for Satan to deceive us.

Yes, according to the Bible, life does go on beyond the grave. For those who belong to Jesus, a wonderful time of reunion will take place in heaven. But until the time has come to join your departed loved ones there, the best thing you can do is content yourself with your wonderful memories of them, rest in the assurance that they are safe, secure, and well in God's hands, and know that you will see them again someday.

7

Hauntings

A Gallup poll reveals that more than 40 percent of all Americans claim to have seen, heard, or felt the presence of a "ghost" at one time or another. These are ordinary people who came face-to-face with something they didn't understand and didn't seek. They weren't trying to contact the spirits of the dead. It just happened.

Strangely enough, nearly one-third of the people who said they had had an encounter with a ghost also said they are "doubters" when it comes to believing in life after death.[1] They know they've brushed up against something really weird, but they don't buy the notion that it was a disembodied human spirit.

Does life go on beyond physical death? The Bible tells us clearly that the soul is eternal and that we will either spend that eternity in God's presence or be forever separated from

Him. Is this a valid reason for us to believe that so-called ghosts or apparitions are evidence of survival of the human soul? If not, what are they?

THE GHOST AND THE NINTENDO GAME

Larry and Susan were thrilled when they were finally able to buy a house after more than ten years of living in an apartment. The house in a Pittsburgh suburb wasn't a mansion, but it was twice the size of their apartment and it was great to have some room for their boys, Jason, eight, and Derek, four.

One of the things Larry liked most about the house was the finished basement, which he planned to convert into a rec room. The boys liked the basement, too, and from the day the family moved in they spent a lot of time there playing and watching television.

They also started talking about the friend they'd met in the basement. They called him "the old man." Sometimes Larry would hear his boys laughing and carrying on down there, and when he asked, "What are you guys up to?" they'd tell him that "the old man" was telling funny stories.

Jason was in school, so he quickly made friends in the new neighborhood. But Derek spent a lot of time by himself. Larry decided to help fill the lonely hours by buying his son a Super Nintendo system. He put it in the basement, still in its box, and told Derek he'd set it up for him over the weekend.

The next morning as he was getting ready for work he heard Derek's laughter floating up from the basement. He heard something else, too: the beeps and blips of a Nintendo game in action. When he went downstairs, he found Derek happily playing one of the games.

"Son? Who set this all up for you?"

"I did it myself" came the answer.

"You did?" It didn't seem like the type of thing a four-year-old could do.

"Well . . . not ALL by myself. The old man showed me how to do it."

More than a little unnerved, Larry called his office, told them he'd be coming in a little late that morning, and went to see the real estate agent who had sold him the house. He told the agent all about his boys' encounter with "the old man" and asked if there was anything about the house he ought to know.

After a long moment's hesitation, the agent finally said, "Your house used to belong to a man named Johnson. He was in his late seventies when he died."

"And?"

The Realtor swallowed hard before continuing. "I didn't want to tell you this . . . but . . . he hanged himself. In the basement."

That's the story the way Larry tells it. He also says he thought about selling the house, but after he and his wife discussed it, they decided to stay. They loved the house, so they made the decision to share it with the strange entity, whoever or whatever it is, and strive for peaceful coexistence.

As far as I know, the arrangement is working out. They're not worried about any harm coming to them because they belong to Jesus Christ, and they know there is no spiritual power in the universe greater than His love. And yet there's a serious question here: What exactly is going on in that house and in other similar houses around the world? My first inclination is to look for and believe in natural explanations, to pass the stories off as tall tales for those with overactive, superstitious imaginations. Still, belief in ghosts has been around for thousands of years.

The fourteenth chapter of Matthew tells what happened when Jesus came to the disciples walking on the water:

> During the fourth watch of the night Jesus went out to them, walking on the lake. When the disciples saw him walking on the lake, they were terrified. "It's a ghost," they said, and cried out in fear. But Jesus immediately said to them: "Take courage! It is I. Don't be afraid" (vv. 25–27).

Some of the disciples had a similar reaction when Jesus appeared to them after His resurrection:

> While they were still talking about this, Jesus himself stood among them and said to them, "Peace be with you." They were startled and frightened, thinking they saw a ghost. He said to them, "Why are you troubled, and why do doubts rise in your minds? Look at my

hands and my feet. It is I myself! Touch me and see; a ghost does not have flesh and bones as you see I have" (Luke 24:36–39).

Jesus didn't berate them for being superstitious. He didn't say, "You ought to know there's no such thing as a ghost." While not exactly an endorsement of the existence of some sort of supernatural manifestation, it's interesting that Jesus felt no need to address the issue.

It would seem that, in some way, ghosts exist. But again: are they the spirits of the departed? I don't think so. I believe the evidence points to a number of different explanations, some simple and others quite complicated.

CAN WE REALLY BELIEVE OUR EYES?

Some experts who have studied ghosts and haunted houses have concluded that many such experiences occur only in the eyes and ears of the beholder. In other words, they are a particularly realistic type of hallucination.

Paranormal investigators Jenny Randles and Peter Hough write that ghostly manifestations may sometimes "have their roots in optical illusions or anomalies of perception. The will to believe can often provide its own persuasive evidence."[2]

Among other evidence, they cite the story of a woman named Ruth, who reported she was often visited by the "ghost" of her father. What made this so unusual, compared to other ghost stories, was that her father was indisputably alive at the time.

With the help of psychiatrist Morton Schatzman, Ruth was eventually able to control her ability to "create" realistic hallucinations. She had learned how to conjure up three-dimensional images of other people, and she sometimes had trouble telling the difference between her hallucinations and real people who were present.

In one experiment, Ruth was asked to create an image of her father and get "him" to stand in front of some flashing lights, which were timed to interact with her brain rhythms. Ruth's brain activity was then measured to determine if she could see the lights through the image of her father. The experiment revealed that Ruth did not see the flashing lights at all! It was as if her father really were standing in front of them. The ghost wasn't real, but it was real enough to block her vision.

Randles and Hough conclude:

> These tests show that the brain is capable of "seeing" something that is not there in such a realistic way that it can fool certain perceptual responses. . . . There is reason to suspect that apparitions could at least at times be very vivid hallucinations.[3]

Further experiments have shown that between 4 and 8 percent of us are "fantasy prone." These people have a difficult time distinguishing dreams from reality and may have hallucinations that seem to be 100 percent real.[4]

There's no way of knowing for sure how many ghostly sightings have such logical explanations. But if 95 percent of all UFO sightings can be explained as a misinterpretation of data, it's likely that a substantial number of hauntings are the result of similar misinterpretations.

Other hauntings seem to be related directly to a desire to believe.

In the early 1970s a British researcher named Frank Smyth decided to make up a ghost story, present it as real, and see if there was any response. He fabricated a story about the ghost of a clergyman who haunted a house in London and had the story published in a magazine. It included the address of the house for those who might be inclined to check things out for themselves.

Over the next few years, he received numerous reports from people who claimed to have seen the ghost. Some described the apparition in vivid detail, right down to his clerical collar.

When Smyth revealed that the story was phony, he was flooded with letters from people who insisted he was wrong. They were convinced that they had really seen the clergyman's ghost, and nothing was going to make them believe differently. One such letter-writer insisted that Smyth only thought he made up the story, but that he had actually written it while under the influence of a real ghost.[5]

GHOST BUSINESS CAN BE BIG BUSINESS

Many other ghostly appearances and hauntings seem to be the result of plain old-fashioned greed. There's plenty of money to be made in the ghost business.

Most people love a mystery. We like to be scared as long as there's no real danger involved. That's why so many of us enjoy roller coasters, scary movies, and the chill that creeps down the spine when we hear "true stories" about events that have taken place in haunted houses—houses like the one featured in the film *The Amityville Horror* and its many sequels.

You probably know the story as it supposedly happened in real life. If not, it's fairly typical. (1) A gruesome mass murder takes place in the house. (2) An unsuspecting family buys the house, not knowing its terrible history. (3) When they move in, they are subjected to all sorts of attacks by the malevolent entities that haunt the house—things like overpowering stenches, swarms of flies, sudden drops in temperature, green slime appearing on doors and walls, and objects flying through the air.

The family's ordeal became the subject of a bestselling book and a blockbuster movie, but not everyone agrees on the details. Some people who were supposedly present when strange, awful things took place have since stated they never saw anything unusual.

It's been alleged that the family who bought the house was in desperate need of money. And it has also been reported that the attorney for the man charged with the murders that took place in the house met with the family to get them to say publicly that the house was haunted. Why?

The allegation is that he hoped to convince a jury that his client was innocent because he had been under the control of evil supernatural forces when he committed the murders. The same forces that were now tormenting the new owners of the house.[6]

What really happened in Amityville? Many believe that, beyond four gruesome murders, not much of anything occurred.

The same can be said of one of the most famous haunted houses in the world, England's Borley Rectory, which was built in 1863. The first sighting of a ghost there reportedly took place in 1885. In 1900, the four daughters of Henry Bull, the man who built the rectory, reported seeing the ghost of a nun walking the grounds.

One of the most famous occurrences in Borley was the rearrangement of several heavy coffins in the building's crypt. The coffins reportedly weighed several hundred pounds apiece, but some strange force kept rearranging them, as if they were no more significant than a bunch of dominos.

The building's reputation was enhanced during one six-month period in 1927 when a dozen clergymen and their wives visited the rectory with an eye toward taking up residence there. All of them decided against it for various reasons, which reportedly included strange noises and other spooky happenings.

Finally the Reverend Erick Smith and his wife moved into the house. They managed to stay for nine months. During that time they reported often hearing footsteps and voices echoing through the house when there was no one else there. They also told of seeing a ghostly horse-drawn carriage coming up the driveway and were especially troubled by a doorbell that kept ringing when there was no one at the door. Finally they said they'd had enough and moved out.

At least that's the way the story goes.

The fact is, Borley Rectory owed much of its fame to a psychic investigator named Harry Price. Jenny Randles and Peter Hough write of Price, "That he courted the media cannot be denied, and evidence that he exaggerated and sometimes cheated to hype up the hauntings at Borley seems fairly substantial."[7]

In at least some instances, this is how ghostly legends are born. There may have been some mysterious goings-on at Borley Rectory, but chances are they were magnified and exaggerated with each successive telling, and then twisted even more by an overzealous "investigator." This seems to happen again and again with "ghost stories" and other tales of the type.

This may even be the case with the story of Larry and Susan that we discussed earlier.

Have you ever had the experience of hearing someone describe an event that the two of you attended together and found yourself wondering how they could be so far off target? It is a natural tendency for people to confuse and exaggerate events. That's just human nature. For that reason, it's entirely possible that the whole story is nothing more than a series of coincidences spurred along by an overactive imagination. Perhaps it's true that Larry bought a house and found out later that the previous owner had committed suicide in the basement. Maybe his sons had an imaginary friend they called "the old man," who really was nothing more than a figment of their imaginations. Perhaps events like these began to come together in Larry's mind and made the story much bigger than it really was.

On the other hand, it is also possible that Larry's home is "haunted" by some mysterious entity of unknown origin. After all, there are some ghosts that seem to defy natural explanation. Poltergeists, for instance.

WHAT ABOUT POLTERGEISTS?

Poltergeists appear to be noisy, destructive, and malicious. They are called the "practical jokers" of the supernatural world, allegedly pulling pranks that are frightening and expensive.

Poltergeists have been reported to throw things around, break dishes, and move furniture, and there have been several well-documented cases of such activity.

One of the most famous poltergeist disturbances of the past few decades took place in Bristol, Connecticut, over a two-week period during the summer of 1975. The victims were a couple named John and Susan Sanford and their two sons. During that time, dishes supposedly flew out of cupboards and were smashed on the floor, pictures fell from walls throughout the house, and furniture rearranged itself. The family also reported hearing growling noises and seeing red eyes peering in at them through the living room window.

A photographer named Paul Eno, who went to investigate the phenomena, said that when he was in the house, he felt something like a strong electrical current that made his hair stand on end. When his film was developed, one of the photographs allegedly showed a bearded face looking into the house through a window.[8]

Whoever or whatever was responsible for the strange activity in the house, it didn't last long and it stopped just as suddenly as it had begun—a common occurrence with poltergeists.

Again, no one knows for sure what poltergeists are. Some feel they are "spirits that feed off fear and hate." However, the Bible has another name for spirits of this type. They are called "demons."

And no demon is a match for the power and authority of Jesus Christ.

One woman told me about a terrifying experience she had when she was in her early twenties. She was not a Christian at the time, although she knew about Jesus Christ and the Bible's claims that He is the Son of God who died for the sins of all mankind. She said she woke up in the middle of the night, feeling extremely cold and terrified. Immediately, she knew that something evil was in the bedroom with her. Her eyes flew open and she saw a gargoyle-like creature standing at the foot of her bed. It was like nothing she had ever seen, and she said she will never forget the utter hatred that shone in the creature's vicious, terrifying eyes.

"Jesus!" she cried, "help me!"

Immediately, the creature vanished. Her bedroom was perceptibly warmer and she no longer felt afraid. She remains convinced that this was not a dream or a hallucination. Something evil had invaded her room, but it disappeared the instant the name of Jesus was invoked.

Shortly after her ghostly encounter, this woman began to read the Bible and pray on a regular basis. It wasn't long before she surrendered her life to Christ, and today she is a missionary, serving Him in France.

Another woman tells of being awakened in the middle of the night by a force pressing down on her body. She could see nothing, but she could feel ghostly hands pushing down on her. When she tried to struggle against her attacker, she found that she couldn't move. Nor could she open her mouth to scream. She seemed to be paralyzed, completely powerless against her ghostly assailant.

She was, however, able to pray a silent prayer: "Please . . . God . . . in the name of Jesus . . . help me!"

At that moment, the attack stopped. The pressure lifted and she leaped out of bed, flipped on the light, and saw that the room was empty.

She spent the rest of the night in her living room with all the lights on, but her attacker did not return.

GHOSTS AND THE BIBLE

Occasionally someone will point to what they say are references to ghosts in the Bible. There are two specific passages they cite as proof that ghosts are the souls of the departed.

The first is the seventeenth chapter of Matthew, which tells us that when Jesus was transfigured, Moses and Elijah, both of whom had been dead for hundreds of years, appeared and talked with Him. But as we mentioned before, this passage really has nothing to do with ghosts. God was making an important statement—that the authority of Jesus is greater than anyone who lived before Him—even Moses and Elijah.

The second Scripture cited is the twenty-eighth chapter of 1 Samuel. That passage tells of King Saul's visit to the medium at Endor, who summoned for him the spirit of the prophet Samuel. Obviously Saul was going against God's law by visiting the medium. But in this instance it seems that God allowed the deceased prophet to appear and give an important message to the king. That message was, "You have sinned, and God is going to take the kingdom away from you."

Neither one of these passages has anything at all to do with ghosts or haunted houses. In both instances, the appearance of spirits of the dead was brought about by a sovereign act of God. All human souls, both the living and the dead, are in His hands, not ours.

THE BOTTOM LINE

Although what we believe about ghosts is important, it's not nearly as important as what we believe about the messages that come through them. Remember what we've said before: Don't trust any creature—whether physical or spiritual in nature—if it denies the divinity of Jesus Christ or says things that directly contradict the Word of God.

When it comes to ghosts or any other supernatural entity, it's vital that we test the spirits according to 1 John 4, and recall the apostle Paul's words from the first chapter of Galatians:

> But even if we or an angel from heaven should preach a gospel other than the one we preached to you, let him be eternally condemned! As we have already said, so now I say again: "If anybody is preaching to you a gospel other than what you accepted, let him be eternally condemned!" (vv. 8–9).

In the 1960s, James A. Pike, a bishop in the Episcopal Church, became an outspoken advocate of spirit communication and other occult practices. The bishop became a champion of the occult largely through what he believed to be encounters with the ghost of his son, who had died tragically of a drug overdose in his early twenties.

The "spirit" of Bishop Pike's son reportedly told him, with tremendous regret in his voice, that he wished he could tell his father that Jesus was Lord and victorious over all, but that it just wasn't true. He also told the bishop that even "on the other side," there were pockets of "believers" who still considered Christ to be their Savior and who waited patiently for His second coming. But they were fools, of course, who were humored and pitied by all of the truly enlightened ones.

On his son's "say-so" Bishop Pike turned away from his faith in Christ. Sadly, through his numerous books, articles, and TV appearances, he undoubtedly moved many others away from faith in the Lord as well.

And yet the Bible is clear on this. If anyone—human, angel, space alien, or ghost—tells us that there is any way we can be saved other than through faith in Christ, he is a liar and a tool of Satan and not to be trusted.

I've said before that I don't know what ghosts are. That's true. But I don't believe for a minute that they are the spirits of dead people.

Once again, let me direct your attention to Hebrews 9:27: "Man is destined to die once, and after that to face judgment."

What could be clearer? After we die we are judged, and then each of us is sent to the appropriate place of reward or punishment.

There's no stopping by the house of an old friend to put in some guest appearances or to play a few games on the Ouija Board, nor will be there be any visits to the home of an old enemy to rattle a few chains and raise some goose bumps.

Do you remember Jesus' parable about the rich man and Lazarus? After the rich man died and was judged, he was sent to a place of torment. He begged Abraham to come to him and cool his tongue with a few drops of water, but Abraham couldn't do it.

Abraham told him,

Son, remember that in your lifetime you received your good things, while Lazarus received bad things, but now he is comforted here and you are in agony. And besides all this, between us and you a great chasm has been fixed, so that those who want to go from here to you cannot, nor can anyone cross over from there to us. (Luke 16:25–26)

I believe that a great "chasm" exists between heaven and hell, and between this life and the next. For that reason alone, I won't listen to any creature that says it has come from "the life beyond" to enlighten me. I may not know what ghosts are, but I do know enough not to listen to everything they say!

There's no doubt that the subject of ghosts and haunted houses is a fascinating one. But it's also dangerous. An interest in ghosts can open a door into the world of the occult that is better left closed. A ghost who seems as gentle as Casper may, in reality, be a demon anxious to mislead us regarding what happens when we die—to convince us that it doesn't really matter what we believe in this life. And as Jesus Christ said time and time again, it does matter. It is the difference between an eternity in heaven and an eternity in hell.

8

What About
Near-Death Experiences?

Joyce Evans is alive and living in England. But perhaps no one will ever be able to convince her that she didn't "die" in 1972, when complications arose during the birth of her son, David.[1]

David was delivered through Cesarean section, during which just about everything that could go wrong did. Mrs. Evans' doctor told her later that he considered her survival a miracle.

What Joyce remembers is that she found herself traveling rapidly through a dark tunnel, approaching a bright light at the other end.

"I knew very clearly that I was dying. There was beautiful music playing, the air was filled with it. The light at the end of the tunnel was very bright."

Joyce says, "I can remember thinking, *It's the end of the*

line for you, yet I felt absolutely no fear."

When she reached the end of the tunnel, Joyce was over-joyed to see her father waiting there, smiling at her, looking exactly the way she remembered him from her childhood. She recognized him immediately, even though he had been dead for fourteen years.

"I was so pleased to see him and be with him, and there was an overwhelming feeling of peace and tranquillity," Joyce remembers. But just before she reached his side, he put his hand up to stop her.

"It's not your time," he said. "Go back! Go back! You have a baby who needs you."

Joyce doesn't remember anything further until she found herself regaining consciousness in her hospital room. She was very ill and faced a long period of recuperation. Still, she was happy to be alive. She did not want to leave her husband or children.

"I felt I had been given a second chance. But at the same time I also know that I have seen what death is like, and there is nothing to be afraid of. I saw how well and happy my father looked, and that was very reassuring. But most of all I remember the lovely feeling I had all the time I was in the tunnel."

AN EXPERIENCE SHARED BY MANY

Millions of people around the world say they have had experiences similar to the one Joyce Evans describes. Today we call them near-death experiences, or NDEs. A Gallup Poll revealed that an estimated 8 million Americans have had these experiences, and many tell stories extremely similar to the one told by Joyce Evans.[2]

They, too, remember traveling through a dark tunnel, racing toward a bright light at the other end. They often tell of seeing dead relatives waiting for them in the light. Sometimes they see Jesus or a benevolent being "of light" whom they believe to be Jesus. Then they hear a voice, or someone comes to them and tells them that they have to go back. And the next thing they know, they're back in the operating room, or at the site of the car crash, or wherever they were when they "died."

Most also say that they were disappointed when they were told they couldn't stay. Unlike Joyce, most didn't want to come back. They also report that the experience has changed them forever. They no longer fear death. And finally, many say they understand how important it is to be loving and kind.

One man, interviewed about his near-death experience, said,

> If my wife was listening I would have to tell you that the most important thing that ever happened to me was meeting and marrying her. But the truth is my NDE is the most important event in my life. It changed me more than any other thing. It shaped me. It changed my personality—and even though my wife has been trying

for years to do that, she's never succeeded. Having an NDE is the most profound thing anyone could go through, apart from death itself.[3]

AN OLD STORY BECOMES NEW

Near-death experiences are not new. They've been around for centuries, even though interest in them has been rekindled in the last decade by books such as Betty J. Eadie's bestseller, *Embraced by the Light*, published in 1992.

And even though near-death experiences have been around for a long, long time, it was only a little over twenty years ago that they became really big news, when Dr. Raymond L. Moody published a book titled *Life After Life* in 1975. Dr. Moody decided to write his book when several people who had been resuscitated after "dying" told him about amazing experiences they had had.

Life After Life sold millions of copies all over the world and touched off an intense debate on the nature and believability of such accounts. His book was hailed as a breakthrough, because it was the first time anyone from the scientific community seemed to take the phenomena of near-death experiences seriously. Dr. Moody had taken NDEs out of the realm of myth, folklore, and superstition and made them respectable.

As for Dr. Moody, he was convinced that something very real had happened to these people who had "died" and then come back to life, and he didn't try to explain it away or chalk the whole thing up to imagination or hallucination. He came close to insisting that these experiences were proof of life after death.

In *Life After Life*, Dr. Moody listed several common characteristics of the typical near-death experience. These include:

- An awareness of being dead.
- A feeling of peace and freedom from pain.
- A journey through a tunnel.
- Emergence from the tunnel into a world of light, peace, and tranquillity.
- An encounter with a "being of light" who radiates love and understanding.
- A review of the life the person has lived.
- A rapid return to the body.

WHAT SHOULD WE THINK ABOUT NDE'S?

The stories Dr. Moody collected almost all had one other common element. They were nearly all positive. Barely a frightening moment in the entire bunch.

Certainly it would be wonderful to think that we have nothing to fear from death. Wouldn't it be great to believe we were all going to wind up in a happy place where the sun shines all the time and everything is beautiful? But on the other hand, would that be fair? Could it really be true that it doesn't matter what we believe or what we do during this life?

The fact is this: not every near-death experience is peaceful and serene. Some are downright terrifying.

Researcher Dr. Michael Grosso, who has interviewed dozens of people who have had near-death experiences, tells about a man who tried to kill himself with an overdose of drugs and suffered a massive heart attack as a result.[4] Friends found him and quickly called paramedics, but by the time they arrived, his heart had stopped, he wasn't breathing, and his body had already turned blue.

According to his account, his soul was on a journey to a place he never wants to see again. There was no tunnel, no bright light, no comforting presence. Instead, the man found himself descending into an inferno where horrible-looking creatures grabbed and scratched at him with their claws. He later recalled that he had a difficult time breathing and felt claustrophobic.

Fortunately for him, paramedics got his heart beating again, and he suddenly found himself back in his body. He said he has made significant changes in his lifestyle, because he did not want to go back to that horrible place.

THEY DON'T REMEMBER A THING

Cardiologist Maurice Rawlins, in his book *Beyond Death's Door*, writes,

Before gathering material for this book, I personally regarded most after-death experiences as fantasy or conjecture or imagination. Most of the cases I had heard or read about sounded as if they represented euphoric trips of an anoxic mind. Then one evening in 1977 I was resuscitating a terrified patient who told me he was actually in hell. He begged me to get him out of hell and not let him die. When I fully realized how genuinely and extremely frightened he was, I too became frightened. Subsequent cases with terrifying experiences have burdened me with a sense of urgency to write this book. Now I feel assured that there is life after death, and not all of it is good.[5]

Dr. Rawlins describes the patient discussed above as having "a grotesque grimace expressing sheer horror. His pupils were dilating and he was perspiring and trembling—he looked as if his hair was 'on end.' "[6]

The doctor worked feverishly to save the man's life, and succeeded. As a cardiologist, he is accustomed to life-or-death situations. But he couldn't get this frightening experience out of his mind. That's why, a few days later, when the patient was stabilized, the doctor asked him why he had been so frightened. Had he seen flames or monsters? Perhaps even the devil himself?

But surprisingly enough, the man didn't know what his doctor was talking about. He didn't remember a thing.

Dr. Rawlins writes, "Apparently, the experiences were so frightening, so horrible, so painful that his conscious mind could not cope with them; and they were subsequently repressed far into his subconscious."[7]

Dr. Rawlins now believes, based on his experience with this patient and others like him, that "when patient interviews are delayed in any way, this may allow enough time for the good experiences to be mentally retained and reported by the patient and the bad experiences to be rejected or obliterated from recall."[8]

He has also come to believe that terrifying near-death experiences may be just as common as the positive ones, and reports that some of the patients he has brought back from the edge of death actually do remember a few details of their negative experiences. They recall entering a dark, dim world, where grotesque people lurk in the shadows or stand along the shore of a lake of fire. He says, "the horrors defy description and are difficult to recall."[9]

For some people, the horror has been the realization that they were heading away from God, instead of toward Him. *Beyond Death's Door* tells the story of a woman who was struck by lightning while on a camping trip. She says,

> In the moment that I was hit, I knew exactly what had happened to me. My mind was crystal clear. I had never been so totally alive as in the act of dying. At this point in the act of dying, I had what I call the answer to a question I had never verbalized to anyone or even faced: Is there really a God? I can't describe it, but the totality and the reality of the living God exploded within my being and He filled every atom of my body with His glory. In the next moment, to my horror, I found that I wasn't going toward God. I was going away

from Him. It was like seeing what might have been, but going away from it.[10]

In her panic, this woman says she cried out to God, telling him she would live for Him from now on if He would spare her life. He did. She found herself back in her body, and within three months she had completely recovered.

NOBODY THINKS THEY'LL GO TO HELL

In her book *Death's Door*, Jean Ritchie cites a 1987 study in which modern accounts of NDEs were compared with those recorded in medieval times. Many elements were the same: the feeling of being out of the body, traveling through a tunnel, undergoing a review of one's life. But that study found one major difference, and this was that in medieval times, negative experiences were far more frequent. People spoke more often of seeing demons, devils, and hell.

Why the difference between then and now? One theory: back then people believed in hell. Now, for the most part, they don't. A few hundred years ago, people who lived sinful lives knew full well they were going to wind up in hell when they died. They were prepared for it and in fact expected it. Today, most people seem to have the attitude that "a loving God would never send anyone to hell." We think, "It doesn't really matter what I do. God will forgive me." We expect the pearly gates of heaven to swing wide open for us the moment we die.

It could be that people don't see hell simply because they don't believe in it. This could mean either of two things: one, that the near-death experience is really nothing more than a hallucination the mind creates to help ease the trauma of death, and that it has no real spiritual connection to what happens after we die. Two, that people who are given a glimpse of hell are so shocked and stunned by the sight of something they never believed in that their minds simply cannot retain it.

THE BIBLICAL VIEW OF DEATH

If we believe the Bible, we must also believe in the existence of hell. Jesus taught that hell exists. In the twenty-fifth chapter of Matthew, He says that on Judgment Day, the unrighteous "will go away to eternal punishment, but the righteous to eternal life" (25:46).

He also said, "If your hand causes you to sin, cut it off. It is better for you to enter life maimed than with two hands to go into hell, where the fire never goes out" (Mark 9:43).

The book of Revelation tells us that when the dead are judged, anyone whose name is not written in the Book of Life will be thrown into the lake of fire (see 20:15).

As we can see, the Bible clearly teaches that hell is a real place.

And so is heaven.

Jesus told His disciples,

"Do not let your hearts be troubled. Trust in God;

trust also in me. In my Father's house are many rooms; if it were not so, I would have told you. I am going there to prepare a place for you. And if I go and prepare a place for you, I will come back and take you with me that you also may be where I am" (John 14:1–3).

Jesus also said that on the Day of Judgment, the righteous will be told, "Come, you who are blessed by my Father; take your inheritance, the kingdom prepared for you since the creation of the world" (Matt. 25:34).

The Bible not only tells us that heaven exists but gives clear-cut directions for getting there: "For God so loved the world that he gave his one and only Son, that whoever believes in him shall not perish but have eternal life" (John 3:16).

When Jesus told His disciples that they should follow Him to heaven, Thomas objected, " 'We don't know where you are going, so how can we know the way?'

"Jesus answered, 'I am the way and the truth and the life. No one comes to the Father except through me' " (John 14:5–6).

Even though the Bible says that those who have accepted Christ will go to heaven—and those who have not accepted Him will not—it does not tell us exactly when this will happen, nor does it say precisely what occurs at the moment we die. What it does tell us is that "man is destined to die once, and after that to face judgment" (Heb. 9:27).

Some believe that when we die we go to a holding area,

a place of sorting, to await that judgment. If this is true, it is likely that those who have had NDEs have only experienced the holding area and have not had a true glimpse of their final destination.

In *Beyond Death's Door*, Maurice Rawlins writes,

> It is interesting that all of my patients who report a continuance from one life to another, whether it was good or bad, usually met previous loved ones in a type of sorting place that often had a barrier preventing entrance into a more permanent type of existence.[11]

Of course, no one wants to hear bad news. It would be easy for us to look at all the positive stories and say, "Life after death is just great for everybody!" But we cannot let selected experiences take precedence over what the Bible says. The Word of God is the final authority in everything—especially matters of life after death.

A WORD ABOUT SUICIDE: DON'T!

Incidentally, Dr. Rawlins says there is one area where near-death experiences have been almost universally negative, and that is in cases involving attempted suicide. He tells of a fourteen-year-old girl who tried to kill herself by gulping down an entire bottle of aspirin. As doctors fought to save her life, she cried out, "Mama, help me! They're trying to hurt me!" She also said that those "demons in hell" had hold of her and wouldn't let her go. Later, after she had completely recovered, she remembered nothing of the incident.[12]

In *Life After Life*, Dr. Moody writes,

> A man who was despondent about the death of his wife shot himself, 'died' as a result, and was resuscitated. He states, "I didn't go where [my wife] was. I went to an awful place. . . . I immediately saw the mistake I had made. . . . I thought, *I wish I hadn't done it.*"[13]

Another woman who took an overdose of drugs reported,

> I remember going down this black hole, round and round. Then I saw a glowing, red-hot spot getting bigger and bigger until I was able to stand up. It was all red and hot and on fire. The earth was like slimy mud that sank over my feet and it was hard to move. The heat was awful and made it hard to breathe. I cried, "Oh, Lord, give me another chance." I prayed and prayed. How I got back, I'll never know.[14]

Do I mean to suggest that all suicide victims go to hell? Of course not. God alone is the judge of that. But these experiences seem to back up the truth that suicide is *never* a good solution.

WHAT DOES SCIENCE SAY?

Before we leave the subject of near-death experiences, I think it's important to note that many experts believe there is a scientific basis for NDEs that has nothing to do with life after death. Instead, they feel that such experiences occur when the brain is shutting down during the dying process. They say that the sensation of flying through a tunnel could be the result of the collapse of the visual field in the occipital lobe. Some scientists also believe that the light that seems to shine at the end of the tunnel may be produced by a lack of oxygen.

Dr. Susan Blackmore, of the Brain and Perception Laboratory at Bristol University in England, points out that the visual cortex of the brain is one of the last areas to die, and says,

> The vital cells that normally regulate the activity in the visual sector of the brain—the visual cortex—are seriously inhibited by the increasing lack of sensory information. This destabilizes the normal visual controls, producing stripes of irregular activity. As this information travels between the retina of the eye and the brain, the stripes are interpreted as being concentric rings, tunnels or undulating spirals, light in the center and darker at the edges. . . . The mind latches on to these tunnel images and accepts them as a new actuality.[15]

CHRISTIANS HAVE NOTHING TO FEAR

This side of heaven, there is no way to know for sure exactly what near-death experiences are. The only thing we *can* know for certain is that Christians have absolutely no reason to fear death. We can have confidence in the words of Jesus, who said, "I go to prepare a place for you."

I think of the death of Dwight L. Moody, one of the most famous evangelists America has ever produced. As he lay dying, Moody shouted out, "Earth recedes! Heaven opens before me!" And then, to his son, "This is no dream, Will. It is beautiful! If this is death, it is sweet. God is calling me and I must go! Don't call me back!"[16]

Truly, for the Christian, "Death has been swallowed up in victory" (1 Cor. 15:54).

9

Vampires and Fantasy Games

No book on the dark side of the supernatural would be complete without a look at vampires.

You may be thinking, "Wait a minute. Vampires aren't real. They're pure fantasy—aren't they?"

"Well, yes . . . and no. If we're talking about vampires who can turn themselves into bats, who bare their fangs to suck the life-blood out of their victims, and who can be killed only by having a wooden stake driven through the heart, then you're right: vampires are nothing more than fantasy. But sometimes it's easy to blur the line between fantasy and reality. There may be no vampires, but there are people who *think* they are vampires, and they may create just as many problems and be just as lost as if they really were 'children of the night.' "

The *Los Angeles Times* recently carried this story from the Associated Press:

> DALLAS—"Four teenagers claiming to be vampires went on a drug-crazed rampage, vandalizing dozens of cars and homes, spray-painting racial slurs and burning a church," police said.
>
> "Fascinated by the occult, the teens smoked meth-amphetamine-laced marijuana before going on a spree through the quiet middle-class neighborhood and causing $300,000 in damage Thursday," officers said.
>
> The fire destroyed the office and fellowship hall at Bethany Lutheran Church. Its outside walls were scrawled with satanic graffiti in pink and white paint.

The article goes on:

> The *Dallas Morning News* reported that one teen told detectives that he and the others were vampires. "The teenagers had marks on their arms from sucking one another's blood," the newspaper reported.[1]

Just a week earlier, another story in the *Times* told an even more disturbing story. A seventeen-year-old boy was sentenced to die in the electric chair in Florida after he was convicted of killing a middle-aged couple with a crowbar. Rodrick Justin Ferrell admitted to the murders and said he killed the couple because he is a vampire.

In imposing the death sentence, Lake County Circuit Judge Jerry T. Lockett said the case proves there is "genuine evil in the world." Ferrell was allegedly the leader of a group of teenagers who engaged in orgies and drank blood because they considered themselves to be vampires. Allegedly, the dead couple's daughter wanted to run away from home with the group and had asked them to help her steal her parents' car. She was not charged in the murders.[2]

So . . . do vampires exist? Perhaps not in the traditional sense. But they do exist in the minds and bodies of those whose obsession with the darker side of the supernatural has taken control of their lives.

GOOD DAYS FOR VAMPIRES

J. Gordon Melton, an authority on vampires who wrote *The Vampire Book*, told me that interest in vampires reached its lowest point in 1983. But since then, there has been a tremendous resurgence of interest in "the living dead." Vampires owe their renewed popularity in part to the bestselling books written by Anne Rice. Her vampire-oriented novels are mysterious, brooding, romantic, and very sensuous— with strongly homosexual undercurrents.

Over the last few years, vampire-oriented clubs have sprung up in America's largest cities, many of them catering to young male homosexuals. Go into any of these clubs and you'll see kids wearing capes and fake fangs. Some have even been known to file down their teeth for a more realistic look.

Did someone say, "So what? It's just fun, isn't it? And

what's wrong with that?" At first glance, it doesn't appear to be a problem.

The problem comes when a select few of the kids caught up in these "vampire games" become absorbed by the fantasy and have difficulty telling where reality ends and fantasy begins. Even my professional actor friends tell me that they sometimes get so deeply into a role that they begin to think and act like the character they're portraying. If this is possible for seasoned and experienced actors, imagine how such role-playing can affect impressionable teenagers still searching for their own identity.

Joan Hake Robie, who has spent years researching the dangers of fantasy games and role-playing activities, says that "shared fantasies" are especially dangerous: "Persons who feel inadequate, bored, or alienated from society can be brought into a position where . . . alternative realities are much more exciting and fulfilling than real life."[3]

She says the result of this can be "withdrawal from society, paranoia, and suppressed or expressed hostility."

Do you remember how David Berkowitz, the Son of Sam from chapter 4, got sucked into satanism? He was a loner, an outcast, who just didn't fit in until his fellow satanists welcomed him into their circle. Variations of this story are repeated over and over again in every area of occult experience and practice.

This is especially true in vampirism. A very high percentage of those who become involved in vampire fantasies are abused children and teenagers who identify strongly with victims of fantasy vampire attacks. They are lonely, alienated young people who are simply looking for someone who will care enough to be a friend, or for a way to have some power in their lives. Sadly, as a result, many of them become entangled in the spider web of the occult.

HOW IT ALL BEGAN

Some experts believe the vampire story was first fabricated in the Middle Ages as a means of enforcing proper burial procedures and thus stopping the spread of deadly diseases. According to this belief, if bodies weren't buried deep enough, they could come out of their graves and walk the streets as "the undead," looking for victims.

In short, vampire legends may have started as the result of an over-the-top public relations campaign on the part of the local health department. But there were other, less civic-minded individuals whose actions perpetuated the myth.

For example, the Countess Erzsebet Bathory of Hungary is said to have drunk and bathed in the blood of more than 600 young girls in the belief that the practice would keep her eternally young and healthy.[4]

But the most famous of all vampires, thanks primarily to the novel by Bram Stoker, is Dracula. Stoker based his character on the life of a Romanian prince named Vlad Dracul, a despicably cruel man also known as Vlad the Impaler, who lived in the 1400s. Dracul, who lived in a rural region of Romania called Transylvania, was driven by political ambition. He was a man of amazing brutality, responsible for the murders of thousands of people, including many women and children who were impaled on long stakes. Their bodies were then erected on roads around his castle as a warning to others who dared to challenge his authority. Interestingly enough, research also indicates that he was a student of the occult.

Manuela Dunn Mascetti, in her book *Vampire: A Complete Guide to the World of the Undead*, writes,

> Dracul decapitated, cut off noses, ears, sexual organs, limbs; he nailed hats to heads; he blinded, strangled, hanged, burned, boiled, skinned, roasted, hacked, and buried alive. It is suspected that he practiced cannibalism himself, eating the limbs of those he killed, and drinking their blood; it has been proven that he forced others to eat human flesh.[5]

Dracul reportedly killed somewhere between 40,000 and 100,000 people during his lifetime. No wonder he came to be regarded as a supernatural monster. Even after his death, peasants in the surrounding countryside were afraid of him. What if Dracul weren't really dead, but merely looking for a new way to spy upon and punish those who spoke out against him? Or, worse yet, what if his spirit were still roaming the Transylvanian countryside, looking for more victims to satisfy his bloodlust?

It's doubtful most teens caught up in vampires are interested in such history. As I've said before, the majority simply want to be loved and accepted or merely have a "good time."

Still, it's always interesting (and sometimes chilling) to uncover the roots of such practices.

WHAT ABOUT OTHER FANTASIES?

We've seen that vampire fantasies can be dangerous. But what about other types of fantasies? Can they be harmful, too? After all, we all have our daydreams. Is it really wrong to leave the real world behind for a while?

Psychologists tell us that it all depends on what we fantasize about and how real our fantasies become. They also say that when a person spends too much time in a fantasy world, it becomes harder to distinguish the real world from the false one.

Some experts believe there is particular danger in role-playing games such as Dungeons and Dragons. These games invite their users into a fantasy world that incorporates many occult-based elements.

When I began to hear people complain about games like Dungeons and Dragons, my first reaction was, "Give me a break. It's just a game." But when some kids I knew became obsessed with the game—lost in its world of magic, wizards, and warlocks—I began to take it a bit more seriously.

We've already seen how Satan will use any means available to lure people into his realm. And, according to Dr. Gary North, author of *None Dare Call It Witchcraft*,

After years of study of the history of occultism, after

having researched [for] a book on the subject, and after having consulted with scholars in the field of historical research, I can say with confidence: these games are the most effective, most magnificently packaged, most profitably marketed, most thoroughly researched introduction to the occult in man's recorded history.[6]

If that sounds extreme, consider that the National Coalition on Television Violence has linked heavy involvement with such violence-oriented fantasy games to more than 90 deaths. These include 62 murders, 26 suicides, and 2 deaths of unknown origin.[7]

Psychiatrist Thomas E. Radecki says, "While perhaps a hundred young people have been led to murder and suicide, the evidence suggests that thousands have committed more minor anti-social behavior, and hundreds have become desensitized to violence."[8]

Here are a few specifics:[9]

- In New York City, a sixteen-year-old named David Ventriquattro was convicted of killing a younger boy who had played Dungeons and Dragons with him. Ventriquattro told police that the dead boy had taken on an evil role during the game, and that it was his job to "extinguish the evil."
- In Canaan, New York, a seventeen-year-old honor student named Wyley Gates shot to death his father, brother, cousin, and his father's girlfriend after becom-

ing involved in a game he code-named "Infierno," after Dante's *Inferno*.

The list goes on:

- Timothy Grice, a Dungeons and Dragons "Dungeon Master," shot himself to death with a shotgun. According to notes found near the body, he had become convinced that, through his role as a Dungeon Master, he had the supernatural ability to leave his body at will. Therefore, he felt that the shotgun blast would not harm him.

- In California, a fourteen-year-old boy was killed after he asked his brother to shoot him. He, too, was a Dungeon Master who was anxious to test and prove his supernatural powers.

We may try to pass these kids off as emotionally unstable or intellectually stunted, but the fact is that most of them were ordinary people with above-average intelligence.

Dungeons and Dragons isn't an easy game to learn. The *Rules Cyclopedia* contains more than 300 pages full of tiny type with hundreds of rules and tactics to be used in different situations. Fantasy games are much more complicated than chess, for example. So you have to be pretty smart to become proficient at Dungeons and Dragons. But quite a few "smart" people have become so absorbed in their fantasy games that they have lost touch with reality.

That seems to back up the words of Dungeons and Dragons creator Gary Gygax, who said, "You have to pursue Dungeons and Dragons with your whole soul if you're going to do well at it."[10] And that pursuit may lead to dangerous actions.

Psychiatrist Thomas E. Radecki, who was quoted earlier, and who has participated in several murder and burglary trials related to Dungeons and Dragons, says:

> From official investigations, from the adolescent murders and criminal defendants that I have examined, and from my own practice, I have no doubt that these games are causing dozens of deaths, as well as a much larger number of more minor problems. The evidence is overwhelming.[11]

MORE THAN A GAME

What makes games like Dungeons and Dragons potentially dangerous? Perhaps it's their intense focus on occult practices.

The National Coalition on Television Violence also reports that Dungeons and Dragons contains numerous mentions of human sacrifices and the drinking of human blood. Note too that characters can repeatedly be brought back from the dead, and that players may choose to worship one of several different demonic entities.[12]

In her book *The Truth About Dungeons and Dragons*, Joan Hake Robie writes, "Twenty-two different types of satanic demons and evils can be part of the game and there are dozens of spells of occult magic with some of the material lifted straight out of demonology."[13]

She says, "Students who participate in Dungeons and Dragons are laid open to a subtle, but very powerful form of spiritual, mental, moral, and thus behavioral conditioning that is extremely dangerous for several reasons."[14] Some of these reasons are:

1. The game is extremely violent.

The world of many of these fantasy games is a violent place where killing and war are normal. What's more, there is no advantage to be gained from being on the side of good.

Robie writes that those who choose good over evil "are inhibited, while those who adopt evil character traits are free to pursue selfish goals. There are no penalties for evil conduct."[15]

2. Some players become overly involved in the game.

"Players can become so emotionally bonded to their characters that when the character is killed, the player becomes devastated to the point of depression."[16]

Robie writes that many players admit that they spend most of their time and energy either playing the game or thinking about it and planning strategy for their next game.

3. Dungeons and Dragons teaches an occult form of religion.

The game uses magic, the casting of spells, pentagrams, and other occult devices and symbols. Players are encouraged to align themselves with demons or to call upon the help of various pagan gods in order to defeat their enemies.

4. The player may be enticed to choose fantasy over reality.

Many of those who have become obsessed with fantasy games have found it increasingly difficult to handle the responsibilities real life brings them. Some have eventually withdrawn into their own fantasy world and as a result have never fulfilled their God-given potential.

Much of what we're saying about fantasy games like Dungeons and Dragons concerns the thought life of those who play. Experts say it is dangerous even to pretend to engage in extreme violence, casting spells on your enemies, participating in witchcraft, and so on.

Jesus had much to say about the importance of a proper thought life. In the fifth chapter of Matthew, he said,

> "You have heard that it was said to the people long ago, 'Do not murder, and anyone who murders will be subject to judgment.' But I tell you that anyone who is angry with his brother, will be subject to judgment." And, "You have heard that it was said, 'Do not commit adultery.' But I tell you that anyone who looks at a woman lustfully has already committed adultery with her in his heart" (vv. 21–22, 27–28).

You see, what we think about *is* important. We must be careful about any practice that causes us to think about things that are evil or unwholesome. This is why the Bible urges us to "take captive every thought to make it obedient to Christ" (2 Cor. 10:5), and "Do not conform any longer to the pattern of this world, but be transformed by the re-newing of your mind" (Rom. 12:2).

The rising fascination with vampires and the ongoing in-terest in fantasy games—whether their adherents see them as "pretend" or not—is alarming. If the Bible's teaching is ac-curate that what we think about shapes and molds our minds, then we must do everything we can to guard our thought life and the thought lives of our children.

10

Reincarnation: Have You Lived Before?

In India and other Asian countries where Hinduism and Buddhism are prominent, reincarnation has long been accepted as a fact. But for America, it got a real boost in the early 1950s from Bridey Murphy.

It was 1952, to be exact, when a man named Morey Bernstein hypnotized a young woman named Virginia Tighe.

While she was under hypnosis, Bernstein told his patient to go back to the time she was a little girl. In response, she began to talk and act like a five-year-old. When he told her that she was now an infant, she started gurgling and cooing like one.

That's when Bernstein tried something really daring. He told the woman that he wanted her to keep going back, to the time before she was born. I don't know what Bernstein expected, but he says he got the shock of his life when his patient suddenly began speaking in a strong Irish brogue. She told him her name was Bridey Murphy, and that she was living in a small village in Ireland—in the 1700s. She described the house and village in which she lived and told minute details about her life.

There were several more sessions where Bernstein took Ms. Tighe back to eighteenth-century Ireland. Every time, the young woman gave her name as Bridey Murphy. She sang Irish songs and told Irish stories, and all of them in the most convincing Irish accent.

Bernstein wrote about the experience in a bestselling book titled *The Search for Bridey Murphy*, and it touched off a furor. Many people were convinced that Bernstein's story was proof of reincarnation. The study of "past lives" became a hot topic—and big business. And everywhere, hypnotists were finding that what Bernstein said was true. When their clients were taken back through hypnotism to the time before they were born, they invariably told sharp details of what seemed to be previous lives.

WHO WAS BRIDEY MURPHY?

So what about Bridey Murphy? Did she ever really exist? Several newspapers sent reporters to Ireland to investigate, but none of them were able to find the slightest bit of evidence. If she ever really lived there, she left nothing at all to mark her existence. Not even a tombstone.

That lack of concrete proof didn't bother those who were predisposed to believe in reincarnation. Bridey Murphy had become a poster child for reincarnation, and they weren't about to let her go. They pointed out that her story had the ring of authenticity. Where, they asked, could she have learned such exacting details about rural life in 1700s Ireland unless she had lived there?

Apparently, they never considered the possibilities: Books. Movies. Plays. School. Magazines. A neighbor, perhaps.

But according to the *Chicago American* newspaper, the latter is exactly where the "myth" of Bridey Murphy came from—a neighbor. While all of their competitors were in Ireland looking for Ms. Murphy, a reporter for the *American* apparently found her right at home, in Chicago. He discovered that a woman named Bridie Murphy Corkell lived in the house across the street from where Virginia Tighe grew up. What Virginia remembered under hypnosis was apparently not from a former life . . . but rather, bits and pieces of information she had learned while she was a little girl.

HAD ANY STRANGE DREAMS LATELY?

What we might conclude from this is that Virginia Tighe's past-life memory was really the product of what psychologists call "cryptomnesia." Cryptomnesia refers to the human brain's ability to store every piece of information it encounters, no matter how random or trivial that information might be.[1]

Sometimes this information is stored deep down in the sub-conscious, making it possible for us to know things we don't even know we know. Occasionally, bits and pieces of this information may get scrambled together into a confusing mess.

Have you ever had a really strange dream? You woke up and thought, "Wow! Where did that one come from?" But after you thought about it for a while, you could see that all sorts of things that had happened to you during the day had been swirled together into the craziest dream since Pharaoh. I've had that experience many times, and I've also noticed that some of the information and events that made their way into my dream were extremely trivial. I didn't realize they had made even a tiny dent in my subconscious when I first experienced them. Apparently the impact was greater than I had suspected, or I wouldn't have wound up dreaming about them.

Not too long ago, I dreamed I was a doctor working on a primitive Indian reservation somewhere in Arizona or New Mexico. The dream was quite vivid and real. For a few seconds after I woke up, I thought I really was a doctor, and I was even a bit worried about some of the patients I had been treating. Later on, when I looked back on the dream, I could see that it was assembled from fragments of information my mind was trying to process—information from a book, a fund-raising let-ter, a few minutes of a television show, and undoubtedly quite a few other more obscure places.

Now, suppose I had been hypnotized when all of this information was fresh on my mind, and I was taken back to the time before I was born as Bill Myers? I probably would have remembered my days in the Old West, perhaps as an Indian, or as a white man living among the Indians.

This is apparently what happened to another woman, who under hypnosis impressed the experts with stories about her life as Livonia, a Roman citizen of the late third century. Her story was so impressive that it was even featured in a book and a television show.

But a researcher named Melvin Harris started combing through libraries, looking for information on ancient Rome that might have found its way into the woman's memories. He found it in two historical novels written by Louis de Wohl years before the past-life regression. His novels not only contained facts regarding daily life in Rome during the third century, but also included many of the characters and events that had filled the woman's "past-life memory."[2]

Had the woman intentionally tried to deceive? No. Remember, she was under hypnosis. But her hypnotist had asked her to do something that was impossible, which was to go back to the time before she was born. When that happened, her mind apparently latched on to information she had read years before and then "forgotten."

DOES THE BIBLE TEACH REINCARNATION?

There is no biblical evidence to support a belief in reincarnation. But some people, wanting to believe in reincarnation, point to the third chapter of John as proof that Jesus taught it. The passage in question involves Jesus' encounter with Nicodemus, a member of the Jewish ruling council:

> Jesus declared, "I tell you the truth, no one can see the kingdom of God unless he is born again."
>
> "How can a man be born when he is old?" Nicodemus asked. "Surely he cannot enter a second time into his mother's womb to be born!"
>
> Jesus answered, "I tell you the truth, no one can enter the kingdom of God unless he is born of water and the Spirit. Flesh gives birth to flesh, but the Spirit gives birth to spirit. You should not be surprised at my saying, 'You must be born again.' The wind blows wherever it pleases. You hear its sound, but you cannot tell where it comes from or where it is going. So it is with everyone born of the Spirit" (vv. 3–8).

There is not one serious Bible scholar who believes the Lord is talking about anything other than the rebirth process that takes place in our spirit when we come to know Christ. This verse definitely doesn't refer to reincarnation. In fact, the concept of reincarnation is opposed to the core of the Bible's teaching:

- The Bible says that anyone who seriously accepts Christ as Lord is immediately cleansed of all guilt and unrighteousness.

- Reincarnation teaches that the sins committed in the last lifetime must be worked off in the next, until we are finally able to reach a state of holiness and purity.

- The Bible teaches that those who have accepted Christ will go to heaven to live forever with God when they die. Those who have not accepted Christ will live forever apart from God.

- Reincarnation says that we will all live again and again and again here on earth until we get it right.

- The Bible teaches that "man is destined to die once, and after that to face judgment" (Heb. 9:27).

- According to reincarnation, we die again and again. There is really no judgment at all—only karma, which will be dealt with in your next life.

In short, reincarnation is a belief system that has no room for Christ's sacrificial death on the cross. If reincarnation were true, it would mean that Christ died in vain. We have no need of anyone to save us if we can achieve perfection ourselves over a period of dozens or hundreds of lifetimes.

Nowhere does the Bible even hint that reincarnation might be true. Instead, it stresses again and again that every human being is a unique individual created in the image of God himself.

And yet more and more Americans seem to be accepting this imported Eastern belief as fact, including many Christians. In 1984, a Gallup Poll showed that just under 40 million Americans believed in reincarnation. By 1991, the number of American believers had reached 50 million. That's more than 10 million new adherents in just seven years. No other religious belief has grown anywhere near that fast.

A friend of mine, a man who professes to believe in Christ and attends church every Sunday, recently remarked to me that a deceased relative had had a very sad life and that he hoped she would have a happier life "next time around."

When I challenged him on this, he bristled and said that he didn't see anything wrong with believing in reincarnation—after all, "our Lord never said it *isn't* true." My response was that Jesus Christ may not have addressed reincarnation per se, but there is simply no way to square His teachings or the rest of the Bible's teachings with a belief in reincarnation.

My friend's attitude isn't uncommon these days. In fact, several recent books attempt to make belief in reincarnation palatable to Christians. The theme of these books is always the same: The early church fathers accepted reincarnation as a fact, but over the centuries this truth became perverted, twisted, and eventually lost.

Historically speaking, this simply isn't true. And as we've already seen, there is no way to reconcile a belief in reincarnation with a belief in Christ's atoning, sacrificial death on the cross. Nevertheless, due in large part to the books I've mentioned and to the writings of people such as Shirley MacLaine, belief in reincarnation and past-lives regression continues to grow in popularity.

THE PROBLEM WITH KARMA

Besides being anti-biblical, believing that a person is going to pay in this life for something he did in a previous existence causes incredible suffering.

Take the Hindu country of Nepal. When a child is born into a desperately poor family or with a disability or sickness, his neighbors think it's due to some sin he committed in a previous life; that it's due to his bad "karma." No one extends a helping hand. Why should they? If a child is suffering because of bad karma, it's because his soul is being purified, and it would be wrong to try to help him.

When I visited Nepal, I was saddened and shocked to see dozens of desperately poor children living out in the open, all by themselves. When I asked about these kids, I was told they were orphans who had been expelled from their village.

"But why?" I demanded.

The explanation was infuriating. When a child is orphaned, it is considered his fault. Instead of helping him, his neighbors throw him out of their village and tell him not to come back. They think they're being kind. They're hoping the child will go off somewhere and quietly starve to death. Then, once his short, unhappy life is over—once he has atoned for his bad karma—he can be reborn into a better life. These starving children scoop up and eat handfuls of dirt in an attempt to stop the hunger pains that tear at their stomachs. It is an outrageous tragedy, and it is directly due to the belief in reincarnation.

SHOULD WE TRUST HYPNOTISM?

Before we leave the subject of reincarnation, let's go back for just a moment to revisit the whole idea of exploring past lives through hypnotism.

What happens when we allow ourselves to be put into a hypnotic trance? Basically, we're surrendering control of our minds to another person. Some experts believe hypnotism is dangerous for precisely this reason. Scripture exhorts us to surrender ourselves to no one but God.

Researcher Robert A. Morey states,

> A hypnotic trance is the exact mental state that mediums and witches have been self-inducing for centuries in order to open themselves up to spirit or demonic control. Hypnotic regression to a "past life" can easily be an occult experience.

He continues with another sober observation:

> Here lies the ultimate explanation for those "unexplainable" recall cases. In every situation where a person recalled a "past life," and this life was researched and proven factual in even intimate details, and not fraudulent, the person was involved in occult practices. Supernatural knowledge was gained by contact with satanic beings.[3]

Don't get me wrong. I am not saying that all hypnotism is wrong. For me, the jury is still out on this. However, I *am* saying that it is a dangerous area, and that anything that happens to a person under hypnosis should be viewed with extreme skepticism.

I've never been hypnotized, nor do I intend to be, so I'll never know what it's like. But an acquaintance who went under hypnosis as background for a magazine article she was writing on the subject said it was an experience she will never forget.

The hypnotist told her she was sitting beside a clear stream in a mountain setting. She remembered that when he said this, she could see the spot clearly, and described it as one of the most beautiful places she had ever been. Then he told her to dangle her toes in the water.

"I could actually feel it," she told me. "It was cold, and wet . . . it was real!"

But it wasn't real at all. Therein lies the major danger with hypnotism. Besides flirting with the occult, it also blurs the lines between reality and fantasy. It is capable of distorting the truth and making us believe a lie. It can make us think we are beside a beautiful mountain stream when we're really sitting in a sterile office building in downtown Los Angeles. And it can make us believe that we have lived before—in ancient Ireland, or perhaps Rome.

TO SUM IT ALL UP

Half of the world's population believes in reincarnation. But that doesn't make it any less of a lie.

Belief in reincarnation is dangerous for several reasons:

1. It lets people off the hook. After all, according to reincarnation, if you mess up in this life you can always do better next time around.

2. It allows us to disregard the needs of others since, according to karma, if people are hurting, they undoubtedly deserve it because of something they did in a past life.

3. It denies the importance of the sacrificial, atoning death of Jesus Christ on the cross and is diametrically opposed to the Bible's teaching that the only way to obtain eternal life is to accept Christ as Lord and Savior.

Remember what the Bible says? "Man is destined to die once, and after that to face judgment" (Heb. 9:27). Not *many* deaths . . . but *one* death. Not *many* judgments, but *one* judgment.

And there is only one way to ensure that we will pass through this judgment without harm: "For God so loved the world that he gave his one and only Son, that whoever believes in him shall not perish but have eternal life. For God did not send his Son into the world to condemn the world, but to save the world through him" (John 3:16–17).

11

New Age— Or the Same Old Story?

It's hard to believe, but it's been thirty years since radios all over America blasted out a song by The Fifth Dimension: "This is the dawning of the Age of Aquarius."

Today, many people still believe we are entering this "New Age" of love and enlightenment. It is supposed to be an era of spiritual renewal, of magic and miracles.

If so, it isn't getting off to a good start. A few years after The Fifth Dimension took their song to the top of the charts, the world saw the savage murders of more than a million innocent men, women, and children under the Khmer Rouge regime in Cambodia. After that, Idi Amin butchered many thousands of his fellow countrymen in Uganda. And so it has gone. Today, it's rare when the morning newspaper doesn't carry at least one story about a drive-by shooting or some other violent crime.

If this is the Age of Aquarius, you can have it!

Nevertheless, many people still believe a new world is waiting just around the corner, and they're looking to a number of occult-type practices to help usher it in.

Much of what we've already discussed falls under the heading of "New Age"—belief in UFOs, communication with departed spirits, and reincarnation—but we can add to these such other occult practices as

- channeling
- astrology
- witchcraft
- astral projection
- Yoga
- crystal power
- extrasensory perception
- Universalism

We need to take a brief look at each of these, beginning with channeling.

THE GOSPEL ACCORDING TO SETH AND RAMTHA

Channeling is nothing new. It's the same thing spirit mediums have been doing for centuries, giving control over their bodies and minds to unseen entities who then speak through them. As we've seen, these entities claim to be any number of things—from spirits of the dead to angels to benevolent beings from outer space.

The entities speaking through New Age channelers are different only in that they now say they are ancient spirits who have evolved over thousands of years and who have now come back to give us the benefit of their wisdom.

In chapter 2 we discussed the fact that Satan has three favorite lies, which he uses over and over again. These are:

1. Jesus Christ is not the only begotten Son of God.

2. There are many paths to eternal life.

3. We all have within us the power to become like God.

Let's take a look at two of today's most popular channeled entities and see how their teachings match up.

The first of these is Seth. Seth began speaking through a woman named Jane Roberts in the 1960s. From that time until her death in 1984, Roberts produced a number of books bearing Seth's name that have sold millions of copies.

Roberts first began to channel "Seth" when she and her husband were writing a book on extrasensory perception. They were using a Ouija Board to do research for their book, when they began to receive messages from someone who identified himself as Frank Withers. Soon thereafter, Withers changed his mind about who he was, explaining, "I prefer not to be called Frank Withers. That personality was rather colorless. You may call me whatever you choose. I call myself Seth. It fits the me of me, the personality more clearly approximating the whole self I am, or am trying to be."[1]

Seth described himself as "an energy personality essence no longer focused in physical reality."[2]

Most of the books "Seth" wrote were dictated through Roberts's voice while she was in a trance. Writing as Seth, she says, "You are given the gift of the gods; you create your reality according to your beliefs; yours is the creative energy that makes your world; there are no limitations to the self except those you believe in."[3]

That sounds an awful lot like "You have within you the power to become like God," doesn't it? It's also troubling that Seth says that we can all learn to receive wisdom from entities such as himself if we will simply learn how to relax and yield control, to "lose the sharp edges of the physically oriented self in contemplation, and an intense desire to learn. These must be coupled with the inner confidence that pertinent knowledge can be directly received. . . . The energy generated by some such experiences is enough to change a life in a matter of moments, and to affect the understanding and behavior of others. These are intrusions of knowledge from one dimension of activity to another."[4]

It is fairly easy to see how Seth relates to much of what we have already talked about.

Seth's books continue to be popular today, but his popularity has been usurped by the "new kid in town," Ramtha. Ramtha, who claims to be a 35,000-year-old spirit and calls himself "the Enlightened One," is channeled by a woman named J. Z. Knight. Ramtha seems to love the spotlight. He makes numerous public appearances, where he dispenses wisdom to wide-eyed believers who have paid up to $1,000 apiece for the privilege of hearing his hard-to-understand advice. Some of Ramtha's followers have reportedly paid hundreds of dollars to be blindfolded and then asked to find their way out of a complicated maze, which supposedly helps in their spiritual growth.

Ramtha claims to have lived on Lemuria, an ancient but highly advanced civilization that sank into the Pacific Ocean eons ago. There is no evidence to prove that Lemuria ever existed, but Ramtha's devotees believe it completely.

Author Jon Klimo describes Ramtha's appearances:

> Knight goes into a deep or cataleptic trance, calming her body so that "Ramtha," a powerful male presence, can enter. Ramtha speaks in a somewhat archaic, stylized manner, claiming to have been incarnated 35,000 years ago as a spiritual and political leader known as "The Ram," who came from fabled Lemuria into what is now India. . . .
>
> Ramtha's theme is that we are like gods; part of God, yet unconscious of this identity. Nonetheless, we create our own realities within which to express ourselves, against which to react, from which to learn, and in which to evolve. This is a view that is virtually identical with the "Seth" teachings as well as with many other channeled materials.[5]

Like Seth before him, Ramtha insists we must learn to "worship" ourselves:

> The reason that I am here is to tell you how important you are. Because the only way that one enters

into the kingdom of Heaven, 'tis not through the worship of another but the worship of the All. And the only way you can ever comprehend the All is from your point of view. And your point of view is called God and that is where you find Him. How do you think, my beloved people, that you ever become? By following someone else, by worshiping something you never saw and never understood? You become by worshiping you.[6]

Ramtha also seems to claim a special "godlikeness" for himself:

I choose to come back in this fashion in this embodiment as a woman, not to demonstrate that a man and a woman can live together peacefully—they can—but [to demonstrate] that God is both man and woman, equally and evenly. [I choose to come back in this fashion] to not leave you any images that you could bolt around your neck or put up on your wall or carve into stone, because you have always been notorious for worshiping others.[7]

How subtle. Is Ramtha using a bit of reverse psychology here? "Okay, you got me . . . I'm a god . . . but don't worship me. And whatever you do, don't worship anyone else . . . except, of course, the god that lies within."

As we can see from this and other chapters, there is nothing at all new about entities such as Ramtha or about the messages they bring.

ASTROLOGY: IS IT WRITTEN IN THE STARS?

Another favorite practice of New Agers is astrology. Astrology says that our personalities and lives are governed by an alignment of the stars and planets. Most people say they don't put much faith in astrology. But every major daily newspaper in America carries an astrology column and a daily horoscope—and they wouldn't waste space if people didn't read them.

Astrology is basically a form of fortune-telling. Boiled down to its basic essence, it teaches that we are dependent on the position of the stars and planets rather than the grace and will of God.

God himself mocks the practice of astrology when he says through the prophet Isaiah, "Let your astrologers come forward, those stargazers who make predictions month by month, let them save you from what is coming upon you. Surely they are like stubble; the fire will burn them up. They cannot even save themselves from the power of the flame" (Isa. 47:13–14).

Apart from the fact that astrology denies the power of God, there are several other reasons why it simply cannot be true. The most important of these is the basis of the entire belief system—the erroneous idea that the stars rotate around the earth. Moreover, there are disagreements among astrologers regarding even the number of the signs of the zodiac, the starting point in mapping out an individual's horoscope. Some astrologers believe there are eight signs of the zodiac, while others insist there are twelve, fourteen, or even twenty-four.

Obviously, astrology is anything but an exact science.

Some people get hooked on astrology because it appears to work at least part of the time. Of course it does. You'd have to be an unbelievably terrible fortune-teller to be wrong all the time. Besides, some of what happens with astrology may simply be self-fulfilling. Someone may get up in the morning and read his horoscope. If it tells him he's going to have a rough day, he goes to work thinking, "I'll sure be glad when this day is over." He expects the worst and he makes it happen. He performs sloppily on the job, he thinks others are out to get him, and at the first sign of any trouble he throws up his hands and says, "I knew it was going to be an awful day." And little by little, day by day, the predictions start to take control of his life.

But the main reason we need to stay away from astrology is because, like fortune-telling and all the other forms of the occult, God is against it.

WITCHCRAFT

Another New Age practice that is definitely not pleasing to God is witchcraft. Remember Deuteronomy 18:10?

> Let no one be found among you who sacrifices his son or daughter in the fire, who practices divination or sorcery, interprets omens, engages in witchcraft, or casts

spells, or who is a medium or spiritist or who consults the dead. Anyone who does these things is detestable to the Lord. . . .

Again, in Exodus 22:18, God commands, "Do not allow a sorceress to live." (Older translations say "witch.")

Nevertheless, New Age proponents of witchcraft or "Wicca" say their "religion" has been misunderstood and maligned for centuries. They will also tell us that Wicca is the world's oldest religion, that it has nothing to do with satanism or black magic, and that it dates back to a golden age when human beings were wiser and nobler and closer to God. They say its rediscovery in this day is a promising sign for our planet's future.

It's true that Wicca is an ancient religion, but that doesn't make it any less a perversion of the truth. The same forces who seek to draw people away from God today were active thousands of years ago.

Wicca has experienced a tremendous resurgence over the last couple of decades due largely to growing interest in two important issues—women's rights and concern for the environment. Am I suggesting that there is something inherently wrong with being in favor of equal rights for women or in working for a clean, healthy environment? Of course not. But as we've seen, Satan often takes important truths and gives them just a little twist to make them false. In Wicca, support of women's rights becomes worship of "the Goddess" and *respect for* nature becomes *worship of* nature.

Margot Adler, whose book *Drawing Down the Moon* is considered by many to be the best introduction to contemporary witchcraft, says the basic tenets of her religion include a belief in the divinity of all (there's that familiar message again), belief in many gods and goddesses (familiar message number two), and relative morals. She writes,

> Thou art Goddess. Thou art God. Divinity is imminent in all nature. It is as much within you as without.
>
> In our culture, which has so long denied and denigrated the feminine as negative, evil, or at best small and unimportant, women (and men, too) will never understand their own creative strength and divine nature until they embrace the creative feminine, the source of inspiration, the Goddess within.[8]

Wicca also centers around the worship of "Mother earth" and a belief that the divine is present in every atom of nature. But the apostle Paul writes that God's anger is directed toward those who "exchanged the truth of God for a lie, and worshiped and served created things rather than the Creator" (Rom. 1:25). Those who worship nature are paying homage to the work of God's hands. They need to stop worshiping the creation and start worshiping the Creator.

ASTRAL PROJECTION

Another interesting component of the New Age movement is astral projection, or "soul travel." This is the belief that human beings can learn to project their souls out of their bodies at will. Classes supposedly teach students how to do this through controlled breathing, meditation, visualization, and other occult-oriented techniques.

In preparing for this book, I watched an instructional video from one of these classes. The instructor was laughing as he told his students that soul travel was such a natural occurrence to him that he often forgot to take his body with him. Just the other night, he said, he had decided to get out of bed and go into the kitchen for a snack. It wasn't until he reached for the doorknob and it went right through his hand that he realized he had left his body lying on the bed. His eager young students all laughed, obviously anxious for the day when they, too, would become adept at astral projection.

But is it really possible to treat my body like an overcoat, putting it on and taking it off at will?

In California, researcher Dr. Charles Tart achieved mixed results when he conducted some experiments with a woman supposedly adept at astral projection. She was asked to "travel" into another area to read a number that had been written on a piece of paper, and was correct only once out of four attempts.[9] Not a very impressive result. Dr. Tart did say, however, that on one occasion the woman seemed to be able to read a clock not visible from where she sat. So that gives her two out of five. Forty percent. Still not convincing.

There is nothing in the Bible that specifically forbids astral projection. But if it is possible to judge a philosophy by the company it keeps—in this instance, communication with departed spirits and reincarnation—then soul travel isn't something to try. It's an occult-type experience that if sought after can easily open the door to other, more clearly dangerous practices.

Some who believe in astral projection point to occurrences in the Bible where God supernaturally moved people great distances in an instant. In the eighth chapter of Acts, for example, is the account of Philip's conversion of the Ethiopian eunuch. The Bible says that after the eunuch was baptized, "When they came up out of the water, the Spirit of the Lord suddenly took Philip away, and the eunuch did not see him again, but went on his way rejoicing. Philip, however, appeared at Azotus and traveled about, preaching the gospel in all the towns until he reached Caesarea" (vv. 39–40).

There is no way this can be construed as an example of soul travel. Philip was in one place, and the next moment he was somewhere far away—body, soul, and spirit. It was Philip's entire being that traveled, and not just his soul.

I once heard a man who was a medical missionary to Africa tell about a similar thing that had happened to him. He was in his office catching up on some paper work when some villagers came running in, yelling for him to come quick because one of their friends had suddenly fallen very ill. The missionary grabbed his bag and ran out of his office. The next thing he knew, he was running up to the sick man's hut. He had instantaneously covered a distance of nearly three miles.

The villagers who had come to enlist his help later told him that they had seen him come running out of his house, but that he had then immediately vanished. The situation was urgent, and so God supplied the means of travel.

But again, it was not merely this man's soul that traveled, but all of him. He hadn't sought the experience. God gave it when it was needed.

YOGA: MORE THAN EXERCISE

Yoga is one more component of the New Age package. Some adherents tell us that Yoga is simply a series of exercises and meditations designed to keep the body and mind healthy. It's just a way to stay fit, they say, and what could be wrong with that? On the surface, nothing. But those who have studied Yoga closely say it's more than a way to stay fit. It's a Hindu form of worship.

The Encyclopedia International says that Yoga is "one of the principal systems of salvation in Hinduism. The word 'Yoga' describes the disciplines for self-development, primarily for the realization of God by direct experience." The article goes on to explain that the aim of Yoga is "to realize the ultimate reality. Its end is mukti, release or salvation."

Douglas Hunt, in his pro-occult book *Exploring the Occult*, says,

> Yoga means much the same as the word yoke in English, and it is a system designed to link the human with

the source of his being. In other words, it has almost exactly the same meaning as the word religion, which also is supposed to yoke man to his master.[10]

One wonders which master.

He laments the fact that Westerners don't always see the religious "benefits" Yoga has to offer and that we are "seldom able to look at anything more than the physical or material aspect of anything."[11]

But refusing to look at the religious aspects of Yoga won't make them go away. If someone says to me, "I know Yoga involves worshiping Hindu gods, but I'm not serious about that, so it's okay for me," my response is that I don't think it's wise to go skipping across a field that's been planted with land mines. Yoga is directly connected to false gods, and for that reason it is potentially dangerous.

One of the key parts of Yoga is extreme, mind-emptying meditation, like that employed by Mark, the young man we met in chapter 1. Remember that Mark finally came to realize that through meditation he was "falling into the grip of someone I didn't want to even touch me."

Through practice of the meditation and exercises associated with Yoga, one is supposed to be able to attain such supernatural "skills" as the ability to foretell the future, the power to read others' minds, the ability to levitate, and the power to remember past lives. This is dangerous stuff. When it comes to personal fitness, I think I'll stick to jogging.

CRYSTAL POWER

What about crystals? Are they dangerous?

I had one dangerous encounter with crystals. It happened on the freeway during rush hour. I was almost blinded by sunlight reflecting off one dangling from the rearview mirror in the car in front of me!

My point is that I believe crystals are no more dangerous than your average rabbit's foot or four-leaf clover. But they are big in the New Age world and are supposed to attract positive energy and thereby bring health and luck.

No surprise here. Crystals have been an important part of the occult world for centuries. Every self-respecting fortune-teller has traditionally had a crystal ball that would supposedly reveal secrets about the future.

It's easy to see why crystals have such an attraction. They're beautiful. They're geometrically perfect. They have the ability to break white light into a dazzling display of colors. And they make beautiful drinking glasses. They're remarkable.

But they are not magical.

On a recent visit to the African country of Tanzania, Christian singer Ron Kenoly met a desperately poor family far out in the bush. He noticed that this family suspended a gourd on a string over the doorway into their hut. When he asked if the gourd was a decoration, he was told that it was far more than that. It was supposed to bring the family good luck. Living in an area where there were no doctors or basic services, they relied on that gourd to keep sickness, hunger, and evil influences out of their home.

Isn't that sad? So primitive. So superstitious.

It could just as easily have been a crystal in someone's house in Indiana.

But that still doesn't say there's anything wrong with the New Age interest in crystals, does it? No. Yet the problem is that when someone is looking to a crystal to keep him safe, well, and prosperous, he has given that crystal the place in his life that God deserves and desires. It's become an idol, and God is pretty clear on how He feels about being substituted by idols.

WHAT ABOUT EXTRASENSORY PERCEPTION AND PSYCHIC RESEARCH?

Like the crystals we've been talking about, extrasensory perception or parapsychological phenomena (PSI) and psychic research can be judged by the company they keep. They're usually lumped together with things like fortune-telling and spirit communication. Thus an interest in extrasensory perception invariably leads to an interest in other, more deeply occult matters.

When I was researching my novel *Threshold*, I was amazed at the amount of time and money scientists devote to the study of PSI. The CIA alone has spent more than twenty million dollars over twenty years of research. In many instances the results are quite impressive, proving by science what we already know by faith—the existence of a supernatural world. That's the good news. The bad news is that more often than not these well-meaning men and women enter the world of the occult without even knowing it. I'll never forget visiting one of the top psychic research labs in the world as they carried out an extensive PSI experiment. And there, at the center of their experiment, sat a Ouija Board.

PSI, psychic research, and other dabblings in the occult—regardless of our intentions or intellect—are incredibly risky ventures. And my advice to these folks is the same as to anyone else. Don't get involved. Because if we play with the devil's fire, we'll eventually get burned.

DO ALL ROADS LEAD TO GOD?

There are a number of other beliefs and practices that fall under the heading of "New Age." But the final one I want to discuss is "Universalism," the belief that all religions ultimately lead to God and that all people will eventually be saved. People who subscribe to this belief consider traditional Christianity narrow-minded and divisive. They believe in "different strokes for different folks." But that is not what the Bible teaches.

According to Scripture, there is only one path and one road to heaven, and in the middle of that road stands the Cross of Jesus Christ.

I want to close this chapter by taking a look at some of

what the Bible has to say about that Cross and about Christ:

> God so loved the world that he gave his one and only Son, that whoever believes in him shall not perish but have eternal life. . . . Whoever believes in him is not condemned, but whoever does not believe stands condemned already because he has not believed in the name of God's one and only Son. (John 3:16, 18)

> No one who denies the Son has the Father; whoever acknowledges the Son has the Father also (1 John 2:23).

> "I [Jesus Christ] am the way and the truth and the life. No one comes to the Father except through me" (John 14:6).

> "I [Jesus] am the resurrection and the life. He who believes in me will live, even though he dies; and whoever lives and believes in me will never die" (John 11:25–26).

> God exalted him to the highest place and gave him the name that is above every name, that at the name of Jesus every knee should bow, in heaven and on earth and under the earth, and every tongue confess that Jesus Christ is Lord. (Phil. 2:9–11)

> "Salvation is found in no one else [but Jesus], for there is no other name under heaven given to men by which we must be saved" (Acts 4:12).

You can't get much clearer than that! So what have we learned about the "New Age"? Simply that there is nothing new about it at all. Basically, it's an attempt to take some of the oldest tricks in the book and dress these lies up in shiny new packages. The Bible tells us that Satan is the Father of Lies, and he's always looking for a new angle, a new way to get us to listen to him. The New Age movement is chock-full of his lies, and it's a road that leads not to enlightenment, but destruction.

Looking for Answers

We have come to the end of our brief journey through the occult. I realize that much of what we've done here has merely skimmed the surface. But everywhere we've looked, we've seen the deceit, false promises, and dangers that await those who dare to enter this dark world.

And yet thousands of people are drawn into occult practices every day.

Why? What are they hoping to find?

Most are looking for answers to their questions about life:

- They want to understand why we are here.
- They want to know that there is more to our existence than the day-to-day grind of trying to make a living.
- They hope to find that life does not end with the grave,

and that miracles can and do happen.

The good news is this: It is absolutely possible to find the answers to these questions and more . . . but not through involvement in the occult. At best, that involvement becomes a money-draining deception, full of superstition and double-talk. At worst, it may open up doors to the supernatural that God never intended for us to open and that we might not be able to close.

There is only one place the Lord gives us permission—and even encourages us—to experience a supernatural encounter, and that is through a relationship with His Son, Jesus Christ. And if you are looking for miracles, that relationship is the biggest miracle of them all.

The moment someone enters into a personal relationship with Christ, a wonderful new life begins. A life that will go on forever. A life free from sin, guilt, worry, and fear. A life of joy, peace, and love.

Having a relationship with Jesus is far deeper, far more powerful, and far more wonderful than any of the momentary pleasures the "masters of the occult" might have to offer. It is the most fulfilling experience a human being can ever have.

When we belong to God, we no longer have anything to fear, because His love is greater—by far—than all the forces of darkness put together. If we belong to God, we not only have His love but the assurance that "neither death nor life, neither angels nor demons, neither the present nor the future, nor any powers, neither height nor depth, nor anything else in all creation, will be able to separate us from the love of God that is in Christ Jesus our Lord" (Rom. 8:38–39).

Those impressive promises have been proven true to me and millions of others for nearly twenty centuries.

If you haven't yet experienced such a relationship and it _ds like something you would be interested in, God has /ided a simple plan. On our own, none of us is good _gh or "spiritual" enough to reach Him. He's infinitely _ and perfect. That's why he sent His Son from heaven— _ffer and die for us, to take the punishment for our fail- _. That's the purpose of the Cross—God paying the bill _ur failures. Once that payment is made, we can enjoy _ supernatural relationship with Him that He's promised. _But the choice must be ours. He respects our free will _much to barge in uninvited. We have to ask. We must _Him to forgive our sins through Jesus' payment on the _s, and, just as importantly, we must take the step of giving our lives over to Him and letting Him be our Lord or Boss. Once that commitment is made, He begins pouring His life into us. Not a bad trade-off. My vain, puny, failing life for His glorious, all-loving, all-powerful supernatural one.

If you haven't made that commitment, think about it. Pray about it. Talk to people you trust who have made it. And finally, check out what the Bible has to say about it. (The Gospel of John is a good place to start.)

Asking Christ to forgive our sins and giving our lives over

to Him is a serious commitment not to be taken lightly. But when you make that commitment, your life will be fuller than you can possibly imagine. Because it will no longer be just your life. It will also be God's life.

AND FINALLY

There's always a danger when condensing so much research and information into a single book. At times the evaluations may seem too simplistic, judgmental, or even un-loving. That isn't the intent. But it takes far more love to warn someone when a building is on fire than it does to say nothing, to simply let them sit there and "do their own thing" while the fire closes in on them.

If I've stepped on a toe or if you strongly disagree with any of my conclusions, please do the research yourself. Check out the Scriptures. Talk to other believers or lay-workers or pastors. But dig deep until you get to the bedrock of truth . . . because God thrives on truth. Yes, there will al-ways be accomplished liars and con artists around to deceive you, but if you keep seeking God and His truth, He will be found.

If you have read this and feel that you are too deeply involved in some of the practices we've discussed and can't get free of them on your own, be assured that help is avail-able. Helping set people free is one of Jesus' specialties. Our Lord said He came into this world "to proclaim freedom for the prisoners and recovery of sight for the blind, to release the oppressed" (Luke 4:18).

He also promises to those who believe in Him: "You will know the truth, and the truth will set you free" (John 8:32).

Again, pray, read, seek mature men and women of God for help. Because that help will come. Not necessarily overnight. Usually it's a step at a time. But every time you reach out to Christ for help, He'll be there for you. He's paid too great a price on the cross to ignore you or to let you slip through His fingers. Just keep reaching out to Him as best you know how. He'll do the rest.

He always has.

He always will.

It comes with his all-consuming love for you.

Notes

Chapter One

1. Brad Steiger, *The UFO Abductees* (New York: Berkley Books, 1988), 30–32.
2. Ibid., 32.
3. C. S. Lewis, *The Screwtape Letters* (New York: The Mac-Millan Company, 1959), 3.

Chapter Two

1. Phil Phillips, *Angels, Angels, Angels* (Lancaster, Pa.: Star-burst Publishers, 1995), 1–2.
2. Ibid., 137.
3. Ibid., 103–107.
4. Rosemary Ellen Guiley, *Angels of Mercy* (New York: Pocket Books, 1991), 65.
5. Bill Myers, *The Guardian* (Wheaton, Ill.: Tyndale House Publishers, 1995), 59.
6. Karen Goldman, *The Angel Book* (New York: Simon and Schuster, 1992), 85.
7. Phillips, 102.

Chapter Three

1. John Randolph Price, *The Angels Within Us—A Spiritual Guide to the Twenty-Two Angels That Govern Our Lives* (New York: Fawcett Columbine, 1993), 101.
2. David Spangler, *Reflections of the Christ* (Scotland: Findhorn, 1977), 36.
3. Ibid., 178.

Chapter Four

1. John Charles Cooper, *The Black Mask: Satanism in America Today* (Old Tappan, N.J.: Fleming H. Revell, 1990), 77.
2. Bob and Gretchen Passantino, *When the Devil Dares Your Kids* (Ann Arbor, Mich.: Servant Publications, 1991), 117–118.
3. Ibid., 33.
4. Ibid., 118.
5. Anton Szandor LaVey, *The Satanic Bible* (New York: Avon Books, 1969), 25.

Chapter Five

1. Ruth Montgomery, *Aliens Among Us* (New York: G. P. Putnam and Sons, 1985), 44–46.
2. Dr. Jacques Vallee, *Messengers of Deception* (Berkeley, Calif.: And/Or Press, 1979), 85.
3. Quoted by Dr. Hugh Ross in audiotape *ET's and UFO's* (Pasadena, Calif.: Reasons to Believe, 1990).
4. Ibid.

5. Ibid.

6. John A. Keel, *UFOs: Operation Trojan Horse* (New York: G. P. Putnam and Sons, 1970), 230.

7. Vallee, 137.

8. Ibid., 21.

9. Ibid., 157.

10. Ronald Story, *Guardians of the Universe?* (New York: St. Martin's Press, 1980), 149–150.

11. Ibid., 150.

12. Whitley Strieber, *Transformation* (New York: William Morrow, 1988), 7.

13. Ibid., 73.

14. Ibid., 198.

15. Ibid., 201.

16. Ibid., 236.

Chapter Six

1. Edmond Gruss, *Cults and the Occult in the Age of Aquarius* as quoted in Josh McDowell and Don Stewart, *Understanding the Occult* (Nashville: T. Nelson Publishers, 1992), 86.

2. Ibid., 96.

3. Jon Klimo, *Channeling* (Los Angeles: Jeremy P. Tarcher, Inc., 1987), 198.

4. Jenny Randles and Peter Hough, *The Afterlife* (New York: Berkley Books, 1993), 46.

5. Klimo, 99.

6. Randles and Hough, 47.

7. Ibid., 49.

8. Lynn Picknett, *Flights of Fancy* (New York: Ballantine Books, 1987), 173–176.

9. Randles and Hough, 79.

10. Phillips, 296–303.

Chapter Seven

1. Klimo, 3.

2. Randles and Hough, 112.

3. Ibid., 113.

4. Ibid.

5. Ibid., 114–115.

6. Ibid., 146.

7. Ibid., 143.

8. Ibid., 129–130.

Chapter Eight

1. Jean Ritchie, *Death's Door* (New York: Bantam Doubleday Dell Publishing Group, Inc., 1994), 75–76.

2. Randles and Hough, 226.

3. Ritchie, 20.

4. Randles and Hough, 223.

5. Maurice Rawlins, M.D., *Beyond Death's Door* (New York: Bantam Books, 1978), xii-xiii.

6. Ibid., 3.

7. Ibid., 5.

8. Ibid., 6.

9. Ibid., 45.

10. Ibid., 64.

11. Ibid., 35.

12. Ibid., 94–95.

13. Raymond Moody, *Life After Life* (Harrisburg, Pa.: Stackpole Books, 1976), 143.

14. Rawlins, 96.

15. Phillips, 231.

16. Rawlins, 53–54.

Chapter Nine

1. *The Los Angeles Times,* March 7, 1998, article by The Associated Press.

2. *The Los Angeles Times,* February 28, 1998, article by Donald P. Baker of *The Washington Post.*

3. Joan Hake Robie, *The Truth About Dungeons and Dragons* (Lancaster, Pa.: Starburst Publishers, 1991), 69.

4. Manuela Dunn Mascetti, *Vampire: A Complete Guide to the World of the Undead* (New York: Penguin Books, 1992), 97.

5. Ibid., 150.

6. Robie, 24.

7. Ibid., 57.

8. Ibid., 59.

9. Ibid., 57–59.

10. Ibid., 13.

11. Ibid., 59.

12. Ibid.

13. Ibid.

14. Ibid., 68.
15. Ibid., 69.
16. Ibid., 70.

Chapter Ten

1. Randles and Hough, 196–197.
2. Ibid., 195–196.
3. Robert A. Morey, *Reincarnation and Christianity* (Minneapolis: Bethany House Publishers, 1980), 24–25.

Chapter Eleven

1. Klimo, 30.
2. Ibid.
3. Ibid., 29.
4. Ibid., 299.
5. Ibid., 43.
6. Ramtha, with Douglas James Mahr, *Voyage to the New World* (New York: Ballantine Books, 1985), 275.
7. Ibid., 274–275.
8. Margot Adler, *Drawing Down the Moon* (Boston: Beacon Press, 1986), ix.
9. Randles and Hough, 213–214.
10. Douglas Hunt, *Exploring the Occult* (New York: Ballantine Books, 1964), 138.
11. Ibid.

By Bill Myers

Children's Series:

Bloodhounds, Inc. — mystery/comedy
Journeys to Fayrah — fantasy/allegorical
McGee and Me! — book and video
The Incredible Worlds of Wally McDoogle — comedy

Teen Series:

Forbidden Doors

Adult Novels:

Blood of Heaven
Threshold

Nonfiction:

Christ B.C.
The Dark Side of the Supernatural World
Hot Topics, Tough Questions

Thank you for selecting a book from
BETHANY HOUSE PUBLISHERS

Bethany House Publishers is a ministry of Bethany Fellowship
International, an interdenominational, nonprofit organization
committed to spreading the Good News of Jesus Christ around
the world through evangelism, church planting, literature
distribution, and care for those in need. Missionary training is
offered through Bethany College of Missions.

Bethany Fellowship International is a member of the National
Association of Evangelicals and subscribes to its statement of
faith. If you would like further information, please contact:

Bethany Fellowship International
6820 Auto Club Road
Minneapolis, MN 55438 USA